** <u>STOP & RE</u>

Thank you and congratulations on buying this book. Before you go any further however, I want to share with you the most important message of this book.

I will not make you rich or build a six figure business or reclaim 2.5 hours a day or find your true purpose.

ONLY YOU HAVE THE POWER TO ACHIEVE YOUR DREAMS!

My role is to guide you, show way-points, ask questions that if you answer TRUTHFULLY will catapult you to greatness you cannot ever imagine achieving.

But it will all be for nothing if you do what 99% of your peers will do and that is to place the book on the shelf.

NOW IS THE TIME TO STEP UP AND START READING!

So without putting this book down, spend just five minutes reading the introduction and Day 1 **"Preparing for the journey"**

Just a few minutes to change your business forever...

How to build a 6 figure property
business in your spare time

Cracking the
Property Code

By Matthew Moody

Some Feedback from the First Edition

"might well be 300 of the most valuable pages you ever read in property."

"I think this is for just about anyone at any level. Put it this way.

If you...
• haven't started in property, it will help you plan and find a suitable strategy
• have a bit of experience, a few properties and are looking for another strategy, it's worth a read
• are considering starting a property-based business, it's definitely worth a read
• want new challenges, it might give you some ideas
• have run out of money, there are suggestions for strategies with a low start cost
• are struggling with your property direction, it might help you get back on track.

Cracking the Property Code, overall, is a bit of a cracker!"
Jayne Owner, Your Property Network

"Just a quick note to thank you for Cracking the Property Code. It was fantastic to be put through the paces to thinking through what I want and helping me understand the various avenues to achieve this. I still have loads more work to do on my goals and working out the 12 x 4 and loving it."
Roxanne Brazeau

Disclaimer & Copyright Information

Cracking the Property Code © Matthew Moody 2013. 2014, 2017

Published and Distributed by Wealth Success Alliance Limited

First Edition 2013.

Second Edition 2014.

Third Edition 2017.

This book belongs to

_____

I own a property business!
My company is called

_____

I AM A BEGINNER / INTERMEDIATE / ADVANCED
PROPERTY INVESTOR.

I HAVE £___.____ TO INVEST WITH TODAY.

I WANT TO GET MY INVESTMENT FUNDS BACK
WITHIN ____ MONTHS.

I NEED LOTS / SOME / LITTLE SUPPORT TO
REALISE MY DREAMS AND MAKE MY PROPERTY BUSINESS SUCCEED!

I WANT TO KICK OFF MY PROPERTY BUSINESS WITHIN ___ DAYS.

I WANT TO MAKE £___.____ PER YEAR FROM MY PROPERTY BUSINESS.

I AM COMMITTED TO MAKING THIS HAPPEN BECAUSE IF I DON'T, THEN
_____

THE NEXT 30 DAYS ARE WHEN I WILL TAKE ACTION TO ENSURE THAT
I CREATE OR IMPROVE MY PROPERTY BUSINESS SO THAT IT IS

☐ SUSTAINABLE   ☐ PROFITABLE   ☐ FUN

Signed   *Date*

_____   _____

FOREWOOD TO 2017 EDITION

Dear Reader,

If you have been searching for a book on property, please stop right now!

What you now have in your hand is the golden tome – the keys to endless riches – the antidote to your troubles.

But to ensure you take the necessary action; you need to follow the plan.

Like life, property needs a plan too.

There is little point in just deciding to invest into the property market if you do not have a plan on how you are going to do this, when you are going to do this and why you are going to do this.

That's where "Cracking the Property Code" comes in.

This book has affectionately been called an "encyclopedia of property investment" by many people and its now in your hands.

They say with "great power comes great responsibility" and I'd thus encourage you to take the reading and subsequent action demanded from this book with care and attention.

The property market has again changed since my last edition and will continue to do so as we traverse across this century.

I've updated relevant passages and added in new content on strategies that have become popular.

But the principles and mechanics still remain the same and with the right approach, mindset and attitude, its possible to do very well from property.

In fact, my mission is to help as many people as I can to achieve financial freedom and security through property.

Will you be one of my success stories?

Only time will tell but I wish you the best of luck and re-iterate:

Follow the plan!

To your Wealth, Health and Success through Property!

Matthew Moody

Northampton 2017

My thanks to friends and colleagues for always challenging me to do better including Vincent Wong, Andrew Knowles, Divian Mistry, Nick James, Paul Avins and Peter Anthony and all the staff at Wealth Success Alliance.

FOREWOOD TO 2014 REVISION

Since I first released the first edition of the book in 2013, things have changed even since then.

Property investing has suddenly become back in vogue, house prices are on the rise and now everybody wants to be in property.

But how do you go about building a business that actually delivers a six figure income for you year upon year and secures your financial future?

When I'd released the book last year, I realised that I had had an epiphany and actually everything that I had been talking about could be wrapped up within a very simple 5-stage process.

In fact, unknowingly I'd been using this very same 5-stage process over-and-over again in my business life to build and sell six figure businesses across the world.

It has been instrumental in me:

- Driving revenues from $2 million through $19.5 million dollars through one product line in less than five years
- Took my portfolio management company managing 50 units locally to a national letting agency managing 550 units from 5 offices
- Acquired £16.5 million pounds worth of lease options and delayed completion stock with rental income of £85,000 per month

- Developed over £1.9 million pounds worth of small terrace properties into 5/6 bed HMO's in Northampton and Leeds for investor clients
- Educated over 2,400 investors through my training company on HMO's and Business Building
- Won Letting Agent of the Year award in our first year of transformation!

And that's not the half of it!

And I put down these results not to boast but rather to illustrate what is possible if you focus and take the right steps to your chosen strategy or business.

However, what I then realised after my epiphany is that although my book was a great start for most people; really I needed to weave in the 5 stages in order for people to make even better use of the materials and techniques to build their own 6 figure businesses.

The "5 Stage Blueprint to Business Mastery" was thus born.

The new revision of the book will take you through each of these stages in a structured manner to allow you to:

- Start creating your six figure business from scratch if you are just getting started (3 to 5 years to attain this)
- Adapt and re-start your existing business so that you can boost your income and start making six figures within the next 12-24 months

With these techniques comes certainty and security that if you implement them, you will truly become successful.

The other realisation I came to is that not everybody will take action (less than 10%) and whilst that's disappointing, I then have to ask myself why this is.

And it's because of the spirit of our own ego's stopping us from achieving what we are really capable of doing.

A good friend and mentor showed me how this result could be taken up to a much higher level through certain key action phrases and hence, this book is also a test to ascertain how these key action phrases can positively influence people to take *some* action and just go out there and do it!

I hope that you'll be part of the action-takers and really start to build your six figure property business and I look forward to continuing the journey with you.

Keep Taking Action Every Day!

Matthew

Northampton, April 2014.

FOREWORD

The idea for this book first came to me whilst I was in Madrid taking some time out for rest and relaxation. I'd been looking for inspirational books on business and property and couldn't find one.

I'd been toying for a while with the idea of writing a book and several ideas had crossed my mind. Several attempts at starting one had been made, but none felt quite right.

They weren't really communicating the message I wanted to get out there.

So I decided that to make my book happen I had to take massive action every single day so I actually ended up with a book rather than a series of random entries and false starts.

October 18th 2012 is when it started for me in getting this book ready and available by 1st June 2013. I know you need and want what's coming up in the next couple of hundred pages, to help you build a successful and sustainable property portfolio.

This book isn't a property and business bible.

It's a playbook to help you become the person you're meant to be, to realise your dreams and take control of your future.

It's here to help you give your all and make a big difference to your life and the lives of those around you, both now and in the future. It's about taking that next step forward to not just being in property and business but being an entrepreneur and taking that energy to be vastly most productive and at peace with yourself.

Some of us never make it but it's one of my missions in life to enable people to realise who they are meant to be and where they are going with everything I've learnt at the coal face of property in the last decade.

Some will say mind-set doesn't matter. I'd counter that by saying what you think makes everything in your life happen.

The mind doesn't understand the difference between reality and the dream world; it just makes things happen as we move through the waking and sleeping hours.

What you believe is your reality.

An old mentor of mine Sunil Jaiswall once said:

Impossible is only an opinion.

I truly believe that. For most people in this country, buying a property is now out of their reach. They wouldn't believe it if you said you could buy a property for very little or no money, and then leverage your money further.

For most people, owning property worth several million pounds is a dream they can merely aspire to.

I'm here to tell you any dream can become reality by understanding who you are and where you want to go -

and then taking action every day towards those goals by making small steps.

Mike Filsaime once told me about the butterfly effect, that a few small changes can add up to a dramatic effect in your business.

I truly believe this and every day we make small changes in my businesses to enable us to keep on top of the market and make a difference to people's lives.

A small change today makes a huge difference tomorrow.

Some of the things I talk about in the book you may have heard before. I'm big on action so I've included worksheets, planners and tools to enable you to take action. To help you further I've put additional tools and planners online for you to use available at www.crackingthepropertycode.com/bookbonuses101

You will need to download the workbook at this url in order to best use the book – so do this right now!

This book is designed to be an interactive journey so it's important you read the book with a pen handy.

I am super excited about this journey we are about to undertake and it's my belief that at the end of this 30-day journey you'll be a more enabled entrepreneur who can take action in the property world and make a difference to those around you.

If you take action on just 10% of what I teach it will make a big difference in your life. Even if you can't directly attribute it all to what I teach, remember this old story:

When you are ready, the teacher will appear and the way will be shown to you.

Together we can create a new breed of property entrepreneurs with a social conscience, who work together to make a difference in their local communities and make the effort to live their lives with passion.

As you go through this book you may see various influences on me that drip out onto the page and I make no excuses for this.

I want to acknowledge some people that have hard-coded themselves onto my DNA and made me the person I am today.

The list is long but by no means exhaustive but for those who want to read everything, I've included a nice bibliography in the back where I've quoted people and books in which you might be interested.

Inspirational people for me include Robert Kiyosaki, Dolf de Roos, Tony Robbins, Michael E Gerber, Timothy Ferris, Andy Shaw, Roger Hamilton, Alan Sugar, Mike Filsaime, Donald Trump, Jay Conrad Levinson, Robert Allen, Victor Hansen, Rhonda Byrne and many more.

How to proceed

As you go through this book there will be exercises to do and while there will be many you will grasp right away, some might not make much sense straight away.

Try them all. This stretches your mind and allows your brain to make certain connections to other material elsewhere in this book.

You may think some things I share don't make sense in isolation, but they will as part of the bigger picture that will gradually be revealed as you make your way through the book.

Two ways to read this book

1) As I the author and concept creator intended
2) Your way.

You can dip in and out of the book and the sections you wish to choose to read, but I believe you'll get the greatest value by reading it sequentially for a thorough process of education, entertainment and action steps enabling you to write your own story and walk your own path.

The book is divided into sections corresponding to certain building blocks you need to create and run a property business and live your life as an entrepreneur.

It's a 30-day process supported by audio and video files on my website (details provided earlier in this chapter).

To maximise this book's potential, commit one hour each day for the next 30 days. Come back every day to this book, follow the exercises and take action on every little thing I recommend - even if you think it's crazy.

By the end of the 30 days you will know more than 90% of property investors out there and be able to invest safely and ethically in the right project. Of course you can dip in and out of this book as you wish, but that technique is best left to those who have either been through my live coaching or mentoring programmes, or are already highly successful investors.

Even then, I still maintain that the 30-day approach works best because once you've programmed a habit, it becomes second nature and works for ever.

And who said we are stopping after 30-days?

There may be a bit of blunt or even slightly risqué language used in this book but it's all for dramatic effect. I simply want you reach this book from beginning to end, then get off your arse and do something with it!

Get in touch

I love feedback so please feel free to get in touch at feedback@crackingthepropertycode.com and tell me how you're getting on.

To your success in life!

Matthew

CONTENTS

INTRODUCTION

Day 1: Preparing for the journey

Journal

A journey has to start somewhere. Why not start with a beautiful new journal?

You may not believe that you have anything of value to share or comment upon but I believe every human being has a story to tell. A life worth living is a life worth recording.

You can write in a journal as often or as infrequently as you wish but I'd recommend getting into a daily habit of writing in your journal at a set time. This way, you ensure that you are getting your journal out and once you get into that daily habit, you will find that your thoughts run clearly on to the page.

Write about whatever you wish, but often it's worth considering what you wish your journal to be.

Do you wish your journal to be

- a record of your daily life?
- a catalogue of your dreams and desires?
- a commentary upon the modern world?
- a place to capture ideas, thoughts and inspiration?

There's so much a journal can give you. You may wish yours to be a combination of the above. Just make sure you have at least one.

Choose a journal containing plain white paper, rather than lined. You'll find it much easier to use – trust me on this.

Where to find the most amazing journals?

Most good stationer will stock a journal but particular favourite brands of mine include Moleskine, Da Vinci, Leuchtturn, Sorrento to name a few.

Pen

Invest in a decent quality pen.

The difference between using a quality pen and a mass produced cheap pen are immense. I have a selection of great fountain pens and roller balls that I use when I want to note down my thoughts in my journal.

You will find the added impetus to writing more if you have a decent instrument to write with!

Favoured brands include Parker, Mont Blanc, Lamy and Waterman but touch and feel and try some out!

Music

Music has always played a large part in my life and I play several instruments to a high standard. I also listen to music all the time as it has the power to

- Inspire
- Move
- Drive
- Energise
- Change your mood
- Make you sad
- Make you happy
- Help you reflect
- Help you meditate

We'll be using various musical pieces to help you complete the exercises. It's not mandatory, but allows us to connect at a higher level and get to the heart of any issue or dilemma we may struggle with.

For the optimum affect, invest in a complete connected home system such as Sonos and really take your home environment up a level.

Throughout the book, there will be exercises and there will be a music suggestion or two with each of them.

Download these musical suggestions at www.crackingthepropertycode.com/bookbonuses101

CD or MP3 player

You'll need something to play music. You can use your laptop or computer if you wish to do this but often the sound quality isn't great.

You might prefer to use a separate CD or MP3 player, and headphones to drive out any distractions hindering your completion of exercises.

For the best quality, audiophiles will say that original vinyl recordings produce the best and nearest sound to the original master but nowadays CD's are produced to such an accurate quality that the sound reproduction will satisfy most people.

An open mind

Some of the items that I discuss you may not agree with, you may think are barmy or you may plainly disagree.

This is normally your ego getting in the way and if you just identify the feelings you experience when this is happening; you can then enjoy the experience of being opened to new concepts, thoughts and ideas.

Either way, come with an open mind and at the end of the journey you may be pleasantly surprised.

CHECKLIST

I've got the following items to help me with my journey:

- ☐ Journal
- ☐ Pen
- ☐ Music
- ☐ CD or MP3 player
- ☐ An Open Mind

What could you do in the property industry?

Often a lot of investors I speak to are surprised how many different strategies you can follow in the property business. Choice is half the problem - people get side-tracked rather than focusing on one or two strategies and getting really good at them.

Here is the list of strategies we'll be covering in this book, so when you start thinking about your vision and your map, you can create them mindful of what strategies ARE available.

Day 2: Your Journey Starts Here

Music Suggestion: Classical, Film Soundtrack, Emotive

My first question is:

Why the hell are you here?

I know, I know. I can hear you saying I'm here because I've read the foreword, and this is the first chapter.

I hear you.

But let's ask that question again:

Why are you here?

99% of us don't have a clue why we are here. That's alright. If everyone understood why they're on Earth, it would lead to some very interesting times for a whole bunch of people.

I absolutely want you to know by the end of this book why you are here and what you are here to do.

I'm now going to ask you to get out your workbook and note down the answers to these questions and any other exercises as we go through the book should be done in your workbook.

Take one minute to think about this and note down some thoughts in your workbook now!

Done? Here's that the second question:

What are you here to do?

The problem with these two questions is most people don't understand why they're being asked. Those that do get uncomfortable and look for something else to do. They start talking about the football game, or the latest celebrity - anything but face up to the question.

And that's alright.

But unless you take the time out to answer these questions there is no way you can truly implement the strategies I teach you in this book to help you live life the way you want.

So take a minute and write some thoughts that come to mind straight away.

Now if I asked you a different question, I'm sure you'd have tons of answers.

Why are you in property?

☐   I want to make lots of money

☐   It's my pension pot

☐   I want security for the future

☐   I want to leave my job

☐   Other

I bet most of you ticked the boxes about making money and maybe a pension or wanting security. A ton of you ticked the box about leaving your job.

But this is not a big enough reason to want to be in property. This reason is not big enough to pull you through the dark days, and cherish the good days.

Let's ask another question (and even if you don't have any properties, please answer it as if you do):

What part of being a landlord do you love the most?

☐ Finding new tenants

☐ Dealing with tenant maintenance issues

☐ Collecting rent

☐ Chasing over-due rent

☐ Doing your tax return

☐ Refurbishing the last house your tenant left

☐ Organising your paperwork and administration

☐ Social worker

☐ Dealing with neighbours

☐ I don't have any properties yet

I bet you that 99% of you read these last questions and thought – what the f*#k is he on about? I don't want to be a 'landlord'.

But as soon as you've donned the mantle of 'property investor extraordinaire' you've become a landlord.

Landlords have responsibilities and regulations to follow and things to do that are not fun and are not exciting and a lot of the time are frankly dull.

But there are ways you can avoid a lot of this if it's not what you signed up for. I'll show you how as you progress through the book.

And then I'll come back to this question:

Why are you here?

If you've not answered it, please go back and answer it.

Your answer ultimately drives you to taking the next steps and living your life the way you were meant to.

We're now going to get into some of this nitty gritty, and I'll show you how to do this.

Excited? I hope so. You're about to change your life forever.

Day 3: The 5 Stage Blueprint

The starting point of a successful business is a great idea but in order for it to become truly successful, it's important that certain steps are followed in the correct format.

This is where my 5-stage blueprint comes in.

This is a system which I've been using for years in FTSE100 companies through to small one-man band operations right through to global conglomerates and of course, my own six figure businesses.

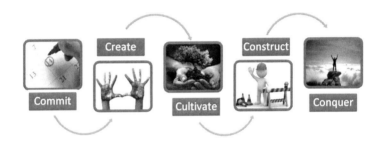

The 5 stages follow a structured order so that you can focus on launching your business whilst covering each aspect of setting up your business correctly at the same time.

The aim here is to generate money whilst your business is being created so you're effectively learning on the job. And if you're already in business, use this as a refresher to revisit your initial ideals of why you set up your business – and is it still working for you the way you wanted it too!

Stage #1 Commit - the beginning of a business and its eventual success or failure is summed up in this very innocuous but brutal reality.

Without fully committing and focusing on your end goals, outcomes and strategies, you will forever be adrift without a paddle chasing the latest wave or boat that comes across your path.

This is in two parts – the act of Committing to a life-long goal and vision and the act of Committing to a chosen strategy or business.

Stage #2 Create - the fundamental act of creating the business is the start. But why stop there.

We can all create yet another business. Why not create an outstanding business that attracts people to it?

99% of businesses are just so-what businesses. Be the 1% that makes the difference and become a make-it big business – one that others want to emulate and copy.

Stage #3 Cultivate - the art of sowing seeds of a business is the start but in order for it to grow, we need to carefully nurture, look after and develop both that business and its clients.

Most businesses get off to a great start but then fail when it comes to continual nourishment and pruning of their business and clients.

This isn't just about your current clients but your past and future clients too and how you manage and work with them on a current and future basis.

Stage #4 Construct - a building without the right structural pattern is a building that will fall down. Similarly a business with no systems is one that will fail due to inefficiencies and duplication, wastage and energy drain.

A successful business will have invested in Systems which are not just digital (ie a operations platform) but are people-led as well (such as a marketing system for collating new leads)

Stage #5 Conquer - if you're going to create a business, why not aim to be "the best of the best?"

Too many folks settle for second best and I just do not see the point. Let's aim to dominate and be the number 1 player in our market place.

The problem with too many businesses and business owners is that they start a business but without a firm plan.

The 5 Stage Blueprint allows anybody to truly Master a Business by following a simple step-by-step process which can then be replicated and used over and over again to both improve, adapt and smash any business.

Throughout the book whilst we are following our 30-day path, I'm also going to break it down into five separate parts so that you as the reader can see how the pieces fit together. I'll share each part of the 5 Stage Blueprint to Business Mastery and illustrate quick wins that you can implement.

Stage #1 of the 5 Stage Blueprint

Commit

STAGE #1: COMMIT

Day 4: Your Map To Success

Music Suggestion: Can You Feel The Love Tonight, Elton John; Free Falling, Tom Petty; Fun, Fun, Fun, The Beach Boys; Gimme Some Lovin', The Blues Brothers

What you'll need

- Journal
- Pen
- Music
- CD or MP3 player

Until you figure out the reason why you want to build a business (whether it be in property or in another field), you will continue to work for "the man" until it's too late and regrets become your way of coping with the disappointment of not making it for yourself.

"Understand Your Reason Why – And Make It Big and Powerful!"

By Committing to a dream, a vision, a destiny, a purpose bigger than you, you will end up following that path and committing to make it a reality.

As part of my 100K Club programme, we work through creating a vision, a life design and a plan that works for my mentees – and it's an extremely powerful shared process to go through with a bunch of like-minded entrepreneurs.

However, there is a second aspect to the Power of Commit that I'd like to bring to your attention.

The Power of Commit only works when you fully embrace it and focus upon one overriding strategy to get you to your goal.

It does not work when you spread your energies, your focus and your passions into multiple areas.

When I got involved with my business, I was a finely tuned machine focused on the next deal and the next property for which to convert into a cash cow. When I had realised my first target however of becoming financially free, I was then pulled and tugged in many different directions over the question of – what next?

This was when I made a huge mistake which concluded in me buying two apartments with a 25% discount (in the days when an 85% mortgage was normal) giving me a huge 10% cashback upon completion. However, the apartments took over 8 months to be rented (due to the availability of flats going up by 2,500 units in the preceding 18 months!) and ended up being rented out for £200 less than the surveyor indicated that they would rent for! This meant that every month I had to subsidise them to the tune of around £400 each to the extent where I had to take a long hard look at whether this situation could continue and sadly it could not so I sold them at a whopping loss just to clear out the monthly payments and pay off the remaining balance over the life of the term.

I tell you this not so that you have pity upon me but that you learn from my early mistakes about the value of commit and that you avoid a painful £150,000 lesson!

The reason why I share all of this with you is because it comes back to the power of Commit. I regularly share stories of people I've met at my live events and one that comes to mind is a chap I met last year who I got talking to at a networking event. When I asked him what he did, he told me that he was in property and when I asked him exactly what he did, he reeled off about 8 strategies – I had to ask him to stop then and re-evaluate his focus and core strategy as without it, he would never make any headway nor meet the goals he had set himself.

Quick win:

Ensure that whatever you do, you are Committed to a Vision that excites you and a Strategy that can generate you enough cash to comfortably live off.

If you want to be successful in anything, you need to follow a vision and dream.

It can't be something you just go along with. You can't simply meander along life's journey living someone else's dream – or helping them live it.

You have to stop right now and get serious with your life.

Nobody else will encourage you to do this because at heart we are all selfish buggers whose primary aim and motivation is ourselves.

I want you to succeed big time but I cannot do the work for you. You actually have to create the dream yourself and take action.

So, let's focus on YOU and your needs and your joy.

A lot of people are so disconnected from themselves that they live in a dream world. They're not truly living life; they're just passive bystanders watching their lives slip by.

I want you to live life to the fullest.

If your dream and vision seem small, that ok. We're going to get to how to make that bigger as we progress and you'll see how easy it is to create an fulfilling lifestyle.

Once you're living that life, you create the flow in your life that enables you to take the opportunities that come your way and start to make those things happen in your life that right now seem to be passing you by.

First I need you to change your state. Get a glass of your favourite beverage and (with the glass on a table) get your body moving by shaking your arms, moving your head up and down, side to side, and rolling your shoulders for 30 seconds.

Done? Now go choose any piece of music that gets your adrenaline flowing and makes you think. The kind of music where you feel the stand up on the back of your neck and you love how it makes you feel.

You should have a few tracks that work for you but if you're struggling, I've suggested some great tracks at the beginning of this chapter.

So, here's a series of questions to answer to get you in the right frame of mind. Please don't' skip this section and please take some time to consider each question but you should aim to finish them all within about 15 minutes.

a) If money was unlimited and time was abundant, what would you do?

b) If you only had 30 days left, how would you celebrate your life and what would be three exciting things you absolutely had to do?

c) What do you absolutely love to do? Who do you love to share these with? Who would you love to share these things with?

d) What are the things that you loathe to do? Who do you dislike spending time with?

e) What are the things that you've always wanted to do but never found the time? What are the things that you think you would like to do? Who are the people you'd like to hang out with that are not in your circle right now?

f) Who are your three major influencers in your life? What are the 3 core things that you've learn from each of these influencers?

g) What is the one piece of advice your parents or mentors would give you if you asked them what they would differently if they have their time again?

h) What places would you like to see that you haven't been to yet or want to go back to again?

i) What gadgets or material things would you like in your life that you don't currently have?

j) Whose life or lives would you like to make a difference to? How would you do it? Why would it matter?

k) If geographical boundaries were unlimited, time travel available and you could teleport yourself anywhere in a heartbeat, describe your perfect day from getting up to going to bed.

How did that make you feel?

I bet you are thinking that that was a serious bunch of questions. And you'd be right. It was, and it is, but it's serious because it's your life and only you can change your life to make it the one you wish to live.

Some of you may have noticed that there wasn't really a lot about property in there. Property is just a vehicle to get you to where you wish to be, but in the vast majority of cases that I've seen, it's not really people's motivation to get up and go in the morning.

The property business may be exciting, and it may be different, and it may be new, but you need to have a vision and outcome stacked up behind this for you to be able to get up every morning knowing that you are going to get out there and MAKE THINGS HAPPEN baby! Oh yes.

Now you've answered these questions, how do you feel?

Are you feeling a little overwhelmed and thinking there's so much I want to do and I just don't know where to start?

Are you feeling I don't really want that much - or I don't really know what I want?

Or are you feeling that exercise was easy and you've tons more to give – so let's get it on?

Whatever the outcome, your journey is your journey and your map is your map.

I run into people all the time on the speaking circuit where I notice somebody that I've seen several times before, they been on one of my workshops and I know from speaking to them that they've been on somebody else's course and it may well be that they are even now on a coaching or mentoring programme because they need help on getting started in this crazy property business because there is so much to learn.

Bullshit! If you are one of these people, you are just deluding yourself and you have turned yourself into – shock horror – a seminar junkie. You are addicted to learning and not taking action.

Anybody can do this stuff provided you take action. A good coach or mentor is invaluable for checking in and making sure you're doing the right thing, but it's up to you to do this - not your mentor.

You'll forgive my little rant there but I really feel sorry for those folks that do go on every course but haven't got started. I know how easy it is and how much further along they would be if they had set out a vision and a plan.

And that's where we come back to.

Without YOUR vision and YOUR plan you are not going to be able to progress.

So I really want to get your vision cemented a little bit now in order to ensure that you get the maximum value out of this guidebook because I am a guide and you are an adventurer and together we are going to go on a journey that has one goal in mind: your ultimate outcome for your life backed up by the power of property.

Take a break now as tomorrow, we're going to crack on with your vision.

Day 5: Your Vision For Your Life

Music Suggestion: Now We Are Free, Lisa Gerrard; Chariots of Fire, Vangelis; The Greatest Day of Our Life, Take That

What you need

- Journal
- Pen
- CD or MP3 player

A life without a vision is a life that will perish. It's a life where you will become the servant of others and not truly master yourself nor your life's path.

You must instead commit to a vision that is:

- Exciting
- Dynamic
- Passionate
- Changes the lives of you and others
- Makes a difference
- Big. Big, big, big.
- Achievable - but only by the seat of your pants

It's sometimes very difficult to actually come up with this vision because most people are too set on living their day-to-day life and slaving for others.

By most people I mean the millions of employees working in a business, the millions of self-employed people doing a job they may love but are in a rut and don't know how to get out, the illusive 'financially-free' who don't actually have a vision for what they wish to do, and so on.

I asked one of my new friends what she did. She told me she was financially free. I asked her again what it was that she did, and wanted to do, and she told me she pretty much did nothing. She didn't have a plan for doing anything much, either.

Don't get me wrong. To be in this position is incredibly powerful, but it's also a waste of the human spirit.

A human is capable of achieving the impossible. Who would have thought even five years ago a human could travel 23 miles above the earth in a balloon, then free-fall back to earth breaking the speed of sound?

Similarly Roger Bannister being the first man to run a mile in under 4 minutes is a feat of the human spirit. His was a story of great determination, to break down barriers and to say no – I can do it. I will set a milestone for everybody else to come after me.

For you to set your vision in a way that means something to you, we need to get in a peak performance state again.

So let's make that change now. There is a downloadable audio track you can download to help you move through this chapter and exercise at www.crackingthepropertycode.com/bookbonuses101

Once again, change your state by getting up off your chair, bed, beach or wherever you are reading this and shake your body out.

Now close your eyes and relax your body, think of your face, your face muscles and relax them, then move down to your shoulders and your arms and your hands and just let then hang and let the tension move out of you, now think of your torso, your legs and your feet and just let them relax.

Now imagine a set of strong cords connecting you with the earth, rooting you to the ground. Imagine a bright white light at the top of your head and let this white light infuse your own body and your heart and really connect with it and let it encompass your whole body.

Next think back to the answers you gave to the very first section when I asked you about if you had the ability to do anything, to go anywhere and be anything, what would you be, where you go, who you would be with, what difference would you be making to people.

Think of this in terms of your property business and where you want to take it and where you want it to take you and what you want it to allow you to do.

Focus on what this feels like, to be living your dreams through the backdrop and benefit of your property investments. Sense what it's like having that cash come into your bank account month after month, experience the sensation of having the time and freedom to live your life on your terms and be the person you want to become.

Make it bright, make it colourful, and imagine yourself stepping into it, living it, breathing it, being the person in your vision.

Now rise up above this vision you have and move three years into the future.

What's changed for you? What are you now doing, who are you with, where are you living, what's happening in your life?

Make it bright, make it colourful, and imagine yourself stepping into it, living it, breathing it, being the person in your vision. Imagine you having the life that you really want.

Now rise up again and go forward five years.

What are you doing now, who are you friends with, who is your lover, what is your business doing, where are you in the world? Are you liberated, happy, successful and financially free?

Make it bright, make it colourful, imagine yourself stepping into it, living it, breathing it, being the person in your vision. Make it as big as you can imagine and become that person.

Now, ten years ahead.

What's changed for you? How has this become reality for you? How has this affected your life? Where are you now? What are you doing? How do you feel? Where are you living? What sports do you enjoy? What lifestyle do you have? Who shares it with you? How are your companies doing? What excites you and keeps you going?

Make it bright, make it colourful, imagine yourself stepping into it, living it, breathing it, being the person in your vision. Make it brighter, more magnificent and become that person, live the life you were meant to live.

Once you have this vision in your mind, come back to down to earth, settle your feet on the ground, feel the connection between you and the earth and then slowly open your eyes.

Now, sit yourself down but make sure you are sitting upright and not slouched over so you keep the energy up. Write down that vision, write down where you'll be, what you'll be doing, who you'll be with, what difference you'll be making, how it makes you feel, what your business is like, what monies are coming in every month, what assets you have to rely on.

Imagine this and commit it to paper in your workbook.

I bet this feels good doesn't it? I bet for the first time in ages you feel truly alive and in the moment. I wager you're feeling so enthused right now you're bursting to start living this vision right away.

But right now, it's just that – it's just a vision. Unless you work on it every day, it will just become the dream that you've had.

What I want to show you is how you make this dream a reality.

But before we do this, I need to share with the strategies that will get you there.

So take a break for now, be grateful that you have finally got down on paper where you want to go and I'll see you tomorrow to introduce the various property strategies – and how you can make them work for you.

Day 6 – 45 Sure-Fire Strategies to Succeed

Let me cut to the quick: digest the 45 strategies illustrated in this book, and choose no more than two or three.

Don't follow the latest craze or movement. Be 100% committed to your chosen route to market.

At the end of the strategies section I'll share the routes I took - and why. You'll also hear about the mistakes I made earlier in not following my chosen strategies.

As this book is aimed at both beginner and advanced investors, I make no apology for including advanced strategies in this book as it's important for you to be aware of them.

Some chapters may be longer than others but resist the temptation to shoot ahead and just read one chapter a day.

Alongside each strategy I've included a key to help you understand whether that may be a wise option for you

The reason I've included this is that often we get excited by a particular strategy and think that ok yes, I'd really like to do that – but we don't really think about what would be necessary for us to implement this – money, support, experience etc. That's why I've come up with a pretty fool-proof key to enable you to choose the right strategy.

The key works like this:

A. Level

This is all about the level of experience you should have as an investor for each particular strategy.

It is a rough guide, but with my 18 years' experience in business I think I'm fairly well versed in advising you here. I've been involved with many aspects of these across the years and have many friends who specialise in certain of these strategies and the one thing I can advise you is that there is a huge difference between wanting to be a developer and being a developer.

There are three levels where you might fit and you may find that you are a beginner in one level but on another level you are at the intermediate level. Let's look at them.

Beginner. If you are just starting out this is a good choice.

Intermediate. Already got some properties, or working in the property business for at least three years? You might like this one.

Advanced. Strategies for those with more than 10 properties or at least 5 years' investment experience.

Beginner	Intermediate	Advanced
✠	✠✠	✠✠✠

B. Funds

This is really where we start to get serious.

It's all very well learning from some guru who's good at sales but short on content how to do a commercial development and earn a million pounds or how to set up a sourcing business and start earning thousands of pounds per month or how to get started in a network marketing business. But every one of these needs funds.

And these funds can vary enormously from less than £500 right up to £1,000,000+

Now every deal is different and clearly the London market is very different from everywhere else but what I've done in this section is take into account the rough amount of funds you'll need.

The total doesn't take into account running costs.

Low - £1,000 to £10,000

Medium - £10,000 to £50,000

High - £50,000 to £199,000

Ultra High - £200,000

Low	Medium	High	Ultra High
£	£ £	£ £ £	£ £ £ £

C. Payback Timing

OK so you've put £20,000 into a specific strategy but what are your parameters for when you want this back?

How do you get your funds back out – and are you prepared to wait?

Some years ago, there was a flurry around "no money down" and how you could acquire a property for no money down (or in) and this would then pretty much equal an infinite return. Those days are over but it's still important to understand the rough amount of time it will take you to get your initial funds back. I chose this over return on investment as this is unique to every deal and an easier barometer to understand for how long your funds are tied up.

3 months - for speedy returns

6 months - for relatively quick returns

12 months - for medium-term returns

59 months - for longer-term returns

60 months or more - for pension planning

3 Months	6 Months	12 Months	59 Months	60 Months
❸	❻	❶❷	❺❾	❻⓪

D. Education or Support Required

The amount of education or support that you will need to follow a certain strategy in order to win. It's not enough to start a strategy if you don't understand the rules, pros and cons, and lack the support if it goes wrong.

Two out of three businesses fail because owners create them with very little understanding of what is expected. When the proverbial hits the fan, they wonder why they fail.

You can take or leave this counsel but I know there are those that have and there are those that want, and I'd prefer you to have what you were destined to receive.

Blue - you should be fine with reading at least three books on the topic, attending at least one networking event in the first twelve months and being on at least one property forum to ask questions.

Red - in addition to Blue, ensure you attend at least one full-day workshops on your chosen subject and join a mastermind group for intermediate to advanced learning. A coach would help accelerate your knowledge.

Indigo - in addition to Blue and Red, it is vital you have a mentor and are part of an on-going coaching and mastermind group to support your journey and plan.

Blue	Red	Indigo
📖	📖 ♟	📖 ♟ ☎

E. Kick off

So you've gone all the way through a strategy and come up with some that you like. But how long will your strategy take to kick off?

If you need cash right now, there is little point going into development or care homes or sourcing a deal as all of these may take months sometimes years to pay you back.

This is all about the time it will take to kick off your chosen strategy and start making money.

This differs by strategy but remember while some strategies take longer than others, the payoff is often far greater.

Be aware of the kick off time and how this will affect your goals.

Kick Off
6 Weeks

This will be represented by the following diagram:

Here's a copy of the key in full as an example of the Buy-to-Let Strategy.

✠ £ £ ❺❾ 📖

Let's get started with the different strategies.

Basic Strategies

1. Buy-to-let (BTL) also known as Single Let.
✠ £ £ ❺❾ 📖

This strategy is the bread and butter of property investors the world over. Essentially, this is where we the investor purchase a house which we then let out to an individual, couple or family.

This can be a flat, house, bungalow or a variation.

The type of market you are aiming for will in some ways dictate where you buy. As a guide, a property close to good transport links, amenities and shops will always out-rent one that is not.

A typical deal will range in price from under £20,000 in the North and Scotland to £400,000 in London.

Yields can vary from below 4% in London through to the low teens in the North and Scotland, depending on the market.

A lot of investors will use a lettings agent to let out their first property and then as they acquire more they may or may not decide to manage it themselves.

This can prove to be false economy but we will talk more about this when we get to the next section.

Cashflow can be anything from £50 to £400 per month although I have yet to find any investor who will show and prove to me that that they own a buy to let which gives them £400 cashflow per calendar month. On paper, maybe, but in reality it's unlikely.

If you aim for £150-200 per calendar month you will be in the right ball park in terms of your forecast.

This strategy is not one that will make you rich, but if you manage your expenses very carefully it could allow you to leave your job, work fewer hours, pay off bad debts or buy some small luxuries.

This is a very good pension strategy. If you buy before your early fifties then you have a decent chance of being able to monetize the leap in value and use this in lieu of a pension.

Use the table at the end of the Strategies section to figure out based on £150 per capita month (pcm) cashflow how many BTLs you'd need to meet your target.

Potential Strategy: ☐ Yes ☐ No

2. Buy-to-sell (BTS)

✠✠ £ £ £ ❻ 🕮

This strategy is where we buy a property with the intent to sell it onto another buyer within a short period of time.

We would typically do this through purchasing a property that was dated, perhaps needed refurbishment work, or was maybe distressed (through a repossession or death). Any of these factors would ensure a cost less than the open market value.

For a BTS property we can quickly establish the difference between open market value and the price we paid. The key is in fully estimating and coming in on budget with the refurbishment costs.

Get this wrong and your profit can disappear overnight.

This strategy often works best when basic remedial work is required, as opposed to a full scale refurbishment (see strategy four). I would recommend avoiding and anything involving structural work.

With this strategy we are essentially looking to add value and then getting our return. It is best to have some understanding of building or to have skills that can be put to use to assist with the refurbishment yourself.

You will need to factor in timeframes for the initial build and then the sell-through which can be through an agent or in conjunction with other strategies (i.e. auctions).

What happens if you can't sell - can you rent it and for how much?

We'd find these deals through agents, newspaper adverts and through our own advertising.

To make this work you need to know the area inside out (even better than following other strategies) because you are essentially banking on your knowledge to buy cheap and sell high.

You also need to have contingency in place in case the build overruns or you cannot sell the property in your expected timeframe.

New BTS operators will be aiming for a minimum profit of £15,000 and this should be your lowest ball park figure in terms of income per deal that you develop.

Potential Strategy: ☐ Yes ☐ No

3. Houses of Multiple Occupation (HMO)
✠✠ £ £ £ ➎➒ 📖 ⚲

HMOs are also known as Multi-Lets or house-shares.

This strategy is where we take a property and rather than renting it out to a single tenant (such as a couple), we rent out each room separately.

This allows us to quadruple our profits and make £500-£1,000 per property, per month.

There are multiple markets and this can allow you to build other strategies around this one strategy through provision of lettings.

However, the market is not without its doubters and challenges.

This strategy is heavily regulated because of the risk inherent in having multiple occupiers who may not know each other or if fellow tenants are present.

The conversion costs therefore can run into the thousands.

Having said that, I believe right now this is one of the best strategies for making regular sustainable residual (not passive) income every month.

Here's one example of a HMO. In Northampton a 3-bed terrace would rent out at £550-595 pcm. As a multi-let, and allowing for just four bedrooms (i.e. no conversion), you'd get £1,200-1,400 pcm depending on the scale of the refurbishment and furniture.

This would improve your profits from perhaps £100 to nearly £300 after all bills.

If you then went and converted say an attic or cellar for £10-20K you could generate an additional £600-800 per month, which would give you pretty much the same in profits allowing for £200 in bills.

Impressive returns, and that's why so many investors flock to the HMO market. But it's important to get it RIGHT and not to skimp on details like furniture, and your setup - and the way you manage the property.

In Northampton, Derby, Huntingdon, Bedford, Manchester and Kettering we manage a ton of HMOs and the quality varies. The better the quality, the more likely you are to rent our your properties quickly and completely.

Aim for a minimum net profit per month of at least £500 and ideally nearer to £1,000 per month.

Potential Strategy: ☐ Yes ☐ No

4. Corporate Lets

❊❊ £ £ £ ❺❾ 📖

Almost the other end of the spectrum; this strategy is where we focus upon the high end corporate lets.

These often work in densely populated major cities or where there is a large corporate employer who often have staff from other countries flying in.

Typical properties can be flats or houses depending on what the client requires. I've rented anything from rooms through to 4-bed detached houses in this marketplace.

Rents can sometimes be a little higher but the service levels need to be up there with the best of the best.

Corporate clients expect a lot and want the very best and can be demanding. But typically especially with overseas posts, they may be looking for 1-2 years so that you can plan your occupancy levels out ahead of time.

Often the company pays directly as well so the prospect of receiving your rent increases further.

Profit levels aim for £250-£1,000 per month.

Potential Strategy: ☐ Yes ☐ No

Day #7 – Intermediate Strategies To Help You Win

5. Refurbishment

⚔ ⚔ £ £ £ ❻ 📖 🔱

This strategy is all about adding value to a property in order to realise profits through changing the fabric of a building.

Sometimes it's difficult to justify this being an advanced strategy as every bloke down the pub seems to be doing up a house.

If you wish to pursue this strategy you must understand what you are doing and move from amateur to professional investor (the difference between this strategy and BTS)

Often an amateur investor will spend all their time working on a refurbishment project only to realise a £10,000 profit. In essence they have worked very hard for this and the actual profit is probably only 10-20% due to the time they have spent on the project, which they never really count.

To refurbish a property is to add value and by adding value, we attract a higher valuation for the property and a better chance of selling this on at a profit.

Do it the wrong way and you can end up subsidising a refurbishment which costs you money.

For a refurbishment to be successful you need to:

- find a house that you believe you can add value to
- find a house in an area that has consistent or rising sales
- negotiate a discount off the asking price (to lock in your equity uplift at the start)
- budget works with a 10% overrun budget
- ensure that you have a full structural survey or use a trusted contractor for a valid opinion on the integrity of the structure
- buy, refurbish and sell on within six months
- aim for at least a 40% margin at the offset (knowing that this margin could rapidly deteriorate if you come across any 'hidden issues')
- have a good project manager managing contractors (budget 6-10% of works for this)
- ensure you understand the local planning laws
- ensure you have building regulations approval for the refurbishment (if necessary) and any other government departments (such as conservation, environment etc.)

By following these basic rules you're a lot more likely to generate money than a scattergun approach with very little supporting planning or proven methodologies.

Potential Strategy: ☐ Yes ☐ No

6. Local Housing Allowance (or LHA)

⚔⚔ £ £ £ ❺❾ 📖 ⚲

This strategy is where we rent out specifically to Local Housing Allowance clients (formerly known as DSS or council tenants).

The strategy has its risks hence why I place it firmly in the advanced strategy as in order to be successful in this area, you need to have an intimate knowledge of the current LHA regulations and have a very thick skin.

Typically LHA tenants will receive an allowance towards their rent. In some cases this may be MORE than the market rent at 100% of its pay-out - but often it is less than the local average rent, so you need to be careful considering the kind of tenant you house.

To find out your local rates for the Local Housing Allowance, go to http://tinyurl.com/ctpclharates.

There are different rates per bed size. Here's how this looks.

Description	Rate Per Week
Shared Accommodation Rate	£57.00
One Bedroom Rate	£80.77
Two Bedroom Rate	£103.85
Three Bedroom Rate	£121.15

Four Bedroom Rate   £161.54

LHA is generally paid fortnightly or four-weekly - so on a yearly basis you might receive 13 payments, and not 12.

The other crucial factor to note is that all LHA is paid in arrears. A tenant moving in on the 1st of the month may not receive their first benefit payment for four to six weeks.

There are ways in which you can speed this up but it is something that you should be aware of.

If there is a difference between the rent LHA clients receive and your rent, make sure the top-up is paid or paid in advance to you to ensure that they do not fall behind with their rent.

The difference between receiving that additional £50 per month could mean the difference between your property being profitable or not.

There is also the question of who receives the rent. Generally this will go to the tenant unless you can prove that the tenant is vulnerable or has money difficulties, and that the rent needs to go direct to you.

Otherwise, the only way of receiving the rent directly is for the tenant to become more than eight weeks in arrears.

Be aware that LHA clients have different needs, desires and outlook on life and thus you need to be comfortable dealing with this client.

There are also caps in place for maximum rent payable dependent upon age, location and house type.

I do not wish to generalise but often you will find that the standard of the house may deteriorate and the circumstances under which they live may not resonate with you.

However these tenants do tend to stay put and if you find the right one, they will look after your property.

Potential Strategy: ☐ Yes ☐ No

7. Lease options

 £ ❸ 📖 ⚲

This strategy is all about control – control over the cashflow and fabric of a building in order to generate short to long term gains.

These operate as a contract that can be used in both residential and commercial real-estate. Lease options can also operate in regards to shares and bonds.

In this strategy a property owner agrees that after a pre specified period of rental you can at the end of the contract decide to purchase the property.

This differs from a lease purchase in that a lease purchase binds both parties to the agreement of sale at the end of the tenancy whereas lease option provides the tenant (you the investor) with the option to purchase, but the seller cannot enforce the sale.

Lease option contracts usually last 3 to 6 years although many that I've done have 10-15 year periods in them.

They operate by the rental-buyer paying a consideration upfront to the owner of 2-3% of the market value (although depending on the deal, you could agree to pay nothing above the consideration of £1; this is preferable to paying a full deposit, as you have the choice not to buy at the end of the tenancy.

An example of this is where a flat is for sale for £180,000 in January 2013. Under the lease option consideration the owner offers the flat for £200,000 come January 2020, for a consideration fee of £1,000. By agreeing to this the investor knows the price of the property will not exceed their reach if the market is to suddenly grow.

If the market drops they have the option to not enter into the contract, but lose the option to buy and search out the market from scratch.

This agreement benefits the investor as you can get out of the property before purchase, and also a deal agreed in advance means that you can build up a stock of units and cashflow before committing to buy.

Benefits for the seller are that they are guaranteed that their monthly PITI (payment, interest, taxes and insurance) payment will be on time during the lease option term; this puts them at relief from their monthly lender. There is also minimal property management involved as the investor generally handles all maintenance themselves.

Furthermore the landlord is guaranteed his selling price if the investor opts to purchase and the transaction is quick as the terms have already been contracted in advance.

An example of this would be on a portfolio I took over in 2010.

We took over a 39-unit portfolio worth £1.45 million. We agreed a purchase price at the time of £2 million within the next 15 years (we had a long time period on this) and a split of rental profits until such time as it was purchased by us. The amount we paid to take over this portfolio was £10 plus our legal costs.

In the end, we upgraded the portfolio and sold it on but it just illustrates the point of how to access property, agree a deal and then take it over.

Potential Strategy: ☐ Yes ☐ No

8. Rent2Rent

 £ ❸ 📖 ♟

This is a way to making a passive income in property investing. The strategy employed here is to take a property from a landlord who is struggling and turn it into corporate accommodation.

Rent2Rent needs to be established correctly in regards to mortgage circumvention, as it can breach the terms and conditions and risk your lender calling in the property loan.

This strategy is often used by investors who want to build up a decent cash pot but do not have the cash to get started with.

It's most often used to rent out properties by the room as this is where the real profits can be made. You'll often find these properties either through letting agents or in the classifieds section of the local newspaper.

An example of this would be a property we rent from a landlord in Northampton where we pay £950 per month and we rent this out to students for £2,000 per month. Even after bills, we clear a solid £500 profit every month.

Potential Strategy: ☐ Yes ☐ No

9. Tenant Buyers

 £ 📖 👤

Otherwise known as Rent 2 own (similar to Lease options), this strategy has massive benefits for the lease option investor.

This strategy generates great cashflow and profit for the owner. It's a simple arrangement where the tenant continues to live in the property and pays rent, but has the option (not the obligation) at the end of the tenancy to purchase the property within a set time period.

Benefits of this for the tenant are they have no need to get a mortgage to start off, and aim of savings for the deposit (or have some of the rent credited for the deposit depending on the agreement) are pre-determined as the purchase price is already pre-agreed.

There is no mortgage application so there is a fast move in for the tenant, and if they decide to buy there's no need for moving costs and time.

The tenant also has the freedom to make the property home, and they get to 'try before they buy'. Moreover, the tenant gets time to clean up their credit and gain lower interest rates, and the tenant can exercise the power to purchase at any time within the time period agreed.

Benefits for landlords are tenants get homeowner mentality which means they're more likely to look after the property and improve it, and less likely to call you with maintenance issues.

Rent is more likely to be paid on time as the tenants' right to buy depends on them not defaulting with their payments. There are further financial benefits as the landlord can collect a rental sum above market value, and they also collect a lump sum (2-3% market value) when tenants move in.

This agreement benefits the investor or tenants over the landlord as the tenant can get out of the property before purchase. A deal agreed in advance saves the house hunting and knowing the price allows time to save for a deposit and for them to be aware of their future financials.

Benefits for the seller are that they are guaranteed that their monthly mortgage payment will be on time during the lease option term, which puts them at relief from their monthly lender.

There's minimal property management involved as tenants view this as their long term home and would rather maintain themselves, with the view of it being their future permanent residence.

Furthermore the landlord is guaranteed his selling price if the tenant opts to purchase and the transaction is quick as the terms have already been contracted in advance.

Potential Strategy: ☐ Yes ☐ No

10. Assisted Sales

⚔️⚔️ £ ❸ 📖 🔒

This strategy is where we assist a vendor sell their property and through our funds and expertise, we make a fee upon completion of the sale.

Here's an example:

A vendor has a property with a mortgage of £100,000. It's valued at £140,000.

The vendor needs to sell quickly because they're struggling to keep up mortgage payments. It could be that a repossession is looming. The vendor is in quite a precarious position but they do not know what to do.

A property professional would ask questions such as:

Does the property need a lick of paint and cleaning up to help it sell?
Is it being marketed properly?
How is it being marketed and by who and for how long?
Is the asking price realistic? Should it be reduced to attract a buyer?

If the property is repossessed the vendors position will be beyond repair and the losses could bankrupt them.

This is where you come in.

If you can position yourself as somebody that can provide the expertise in terms of marketing and refurbishment, then there could be potential profit in the deal for you.

You could arrange to quickly paint the property, tidy it up and then remarket it as a slightly lower price (say £130,000) to leave a balance of £30,000.

This balance can then be split 50-50 or perhaps 70-30 depending on what you and the vendor have agreed.

This is down to negotiation and is entirely flexible.

The paperwork needs preparing by a solicitor in order to protect you and ensure that you are paid from the sale proceeds.

This is just an example of how assisted sales can work but there are many ways in which you could generate income from this strategy.

Potential Strategy: ☐ Yes ☐ No

11. Planning Gains

✠ ✠ £ £ £ ❻ 📖 ⚱

This strategy is all about taking on either options or agreements in place to benefit from planning gains made through applying for planning on units that do not currently have planning approval.

Another variation but one to consider for people who like to have several projects on-going with potential payoffs.

A strategy was often pushed in the late noughties of combining back gardens in order to build a unit or using corner plots to build more units in.

As long as you are clear on the local plan, understand what access you need in order to build and have residents park, then planning gains may be an avenue for you to consider further.

A piece of land which does not have planning permission sells for between £6,000-£10,000 per acre. One with planning permission can go for as much as £1,000,000.

Even small plots can be profitable.

Potential Strategy: ☐ Yes ☐ No

12. Serviced Apartments

✠✠ £ £ £ ❺❾ 📖

A strategy where apartments or houses are rented out on short term contracts or even by the night.

Since the initial book was written, the strategy has become hugely popular amongst property investors in an effort to achieve huge returns on over-priced and over-leveraged stock.

With the recent popularity of AirBnB and other providers, this strategy has become the latest one upon which the "property training industry" has leaped upon with typical profits being bandied around of £2,000 to £4,000 per month.

This strategy has always been particularly popular in London, Manchester, Leeds and Liverpool where huge amounts of flats where built causing an oversupply in the market and thus massive reduction in both demand and rental prices and I remember staying in such apartments in the noughties – some better than others.

How do the figures work:

A 2-bed flat in Liverpool would rent for £700 pcm (there are 1,000 flats for rent in Liverpool at time of writing).

Let's say we rented these out for £60 per night, assuming occupancy during the week of 100% (Sunday to Thursday) and 50% at weekends (Friday to Saturday).

This would give us an overall occupancy rate of 85.7% giving us a monthly income of £1,530.

Assuming cleaning costs of £5 per day plus on costs of £5 per booking, this would give us costs of £255 per month making us £1,275 before any mortgage or insurance payments.

A slight improvement over £700 pcm.

And these gains are entirely possible if you know what you are doing, buy in the right block of apartments and aim at the luxury and corporate let market.

The figures quoted above are also at the lower end of the market so with the right product, it could be possible to double these figures.

However it is not for the faint of heart.

This strategy is the same as running a hotel albeit on a smaller basis and potentially spread out amongst multiple sites.

There is clearly money to be made but the successful investor will spend time and money to implement the correct systems to minimise their time or talking themselves into another "job".

Potential Strategy: ☐ Yes ☐ No

Day #8 – Advanced Strategies

13. Social Housing provides affordable housing to those on low incomes.

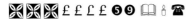

This strategy is where we provide accommodation for people on low incomes through provision of large stocks of inventory.

Rents are kept low through the provision of state subsidy, and this is strictly defined by government controls on affordability. Unlike the private sector where tenancies are offered based on landlord choice, this sector allocates based on need.

Social landlords own and manage social housing and operate their own allocations policy. They state in advance what factors they will be taking into account when deciding preferences of tenants. Beyond governmental outlines set in law, this is at the landlord's discretion.

These bodies are often non-commercial but are expanding to be owned and run by commercial organisations. It is now more common to find social housing being provided by the private sector due to the legacy of the Thatcher years, and as a result of the economic crisis and the government cut of the social housing budget by 50% back in 2010. This is a tightly regulated area, with the government department CLG

(Communities and Local Government) overseeing developments and the running of social housing.

There are currently (according to governmental figures) 1.8 million households on waiting lists for social housing. The government is now promoting low-cost housing schemes to assist the non-commercial bodies in solving this current social issue.

The government has recently introduced a new programme in this area called the Affordable Homes Programme. This programme is projected to be the new main form of housing supply to this sector and allow for the new more diverse range of people now in this market.

These homes will be made available to tenants at a maximum of 80% of market rent, but will continue to be allocated in the same manner it is currently.

The government has made it more attractive to non-commercial enterprises by changing its measures in relations to Tenure, with landlords no longer offering lifetime tenancies in favour of contracts spanning a minimum of two years.

This area has been made much more attractive to the private sector, the predominant social housing supplier, in an attempt to encourage more private investment to tackle the growing need for social housing.

To get started in this market would require a sizeable number of houses or blocks of flats. A social housing organisation would be managing hundreds of units, so it's not something that you can just get started in.

But if you are already at the stage of owning hundreds of units, this may be a strategy which will work for you based upon redefining your legal status and changing your business' focus from private rentals to council tenancies.

Potential Strategy: ☐ Yes ☐ No

14. Overseas - how to buy property abroad.

⚔ ⚔ £ £ £ ❻❿ 📖
This strategy is focused upon generating returns from the lucrative but speculative overseas market.

If you are planning to go down this route make sure you are looking to invest long term to gain a suitable return on your investment.

There are many EU countries where property markets have taken a big hit so now may be the time to invest providing you are clear on legislation in your chosen country (in some areas there are on-going issues with illegal building and land grabs).

If you're planning to let your property when you're not using it, it's important to bear this in mind when you're hunting for your new holiday home.

Make sure it's in an easily accessible location with good local amenities and in an area popular with tourists.

You should also investigate the competition. Find out what the going rate is for rental on similar properties to get a realistic idea of how much you could make.

Don't forget to take into account the holiday season in the area, because many tourist destinations virtually shut down when it comes to the end of the season.

Cheaper marketing options than an estate agent are dedicated holiday lettings websites. Word of mouth through family and friends is another good way to find potential rental income.

But attracting business and managing the property yourself could be difficult, especially if you're in the UK most of the time.

You must pay income tax on rent you receive. You are liable for tax both in the country itself and in the UK – although there are national agreements that mean you shouldn't have to pay the same tax twice. Make sure you have a lawyer look into this before you consider investing in a property abroad.

If you're looking to buy off plan then legal protection is essential. A well-negotiated contract should set out a clear payment schedule – for example, 5% on signing the reservation contract, 30% when foundations are finished, 35% when the shell is weather-proof, 25% on completion of the build and 5% when you get the keys.

 It should also clarify what finishes the developer is promising and provide a comprehensive, bank-backed guarantee stipulating that if the builders go bust the job will be completed to the same standard, at no extra cost to you.

Your lawyer should clarify how any guaranteed rental income or leaseback schemes the developer is offering will operate. These can look good on paper but may not reflect the long-term rental potential of the property.

Five top tips for investing in property overseas:

1. **Choose your estate agent carefully**. Try and get previous testimonials and dig into their history. Read the small print and check their fees upfront. Invest time and money looking at the properties rather than become stuck on your laptop at home in the UK.

2. **Be sceptical**. Always research the claims of gaining a huge capital growth and yielding extraordinary percentages. Look at the maintenance costs, costs of purchase and taxation you are likely to face. Also look at the competition and make sure the property you invest in is going to be competitive enough to have occupancy rates.

3. **Weigh it all up**. Evaluate the pluses and minuses of each property, looking at all the costs (purchase, commission to the estate agent, legal costs, taxation, utilities, property management, cleaning and so on). Look for the best mortgage deals and currency transfers, and always be aware of the potential liability for taxes both in the UK and abroad.

4. **Seek asset advice.** Talk to your lawyer (one you trust and is bilingual with yours as their mother tongue to make sure nothing is lost in translation) and discuss wills in both countries. Once you've found the right property abroad, hire

a suitably qualified lawyer to protect your interests and negotiate a favourable contract (make sure you are aware of the country's purchase laws and terms of the contract) before handing over a deposit securely via a lawyer or bonded agent this way everything is secure.

5. **Do your homework.** If you're planning to emigrate, research your tax, pension and healthcare requirements. If you're below retirement age, carefully consider your healthcare insurance as you may lose NHS rights and need to consider investing in private healthcare.

If you're looking to invest in the overseas market make sure your strategy allows for voids, for refurbishment and that you have properly weighed the pros and cons of doing this.

Managing from afar can work, but you need to have the appropriate systems in place.

Potential Strategy: ☐ Yes ☐ No

15. Auction strategy

⚔ ⚔ £ £ £ ➌ 📖 🗝

Auction strategy is when somebody would be buying properties at auction to either flip or refurbish them in order to sell on or rent.

There is a lot of research and preparation to be done. There are risks. However there are great rewards - the chance to get your first property at a great price, and be set up for life with less debt as a result.

Auctions are one way to get a property cheaper than average price as sometimes properties go for up to 20% less than market value, or better. This level of reduction needs a low reserve from the seller, and little bidding competition.

The other benefits of buying at auction are fast closure, because as soon as the auctioneer declares a winning bidder they own the property (subject to deposit payment and the final balance) with completion normally occurring within 28 days.

This option is much less hassle than normal property purchase. There is also no issue of 'gazumping' (where someone else puts in a bid higher than your offer and the seller can opt to drop out of the deal and take the higher price).

Furthermore there is no negotiating through a middle man (estate agent), no chain and no chance of the sale falling though.

If you are a first time buyer and have no house to sell you're in a much better position to purchase at auction than someone with a house to sell or a mortgage.

Disadvantages? Less choice, as there are fewer properties for sale at an auction than at estate agents, restricting your choice of location.

You must also be aware of the need to renovate completely or at least give the property some TLC.

If you aren't prepared to get your hands dirty there will be very few properties at auction for you to purchase. Timescales are tight as the auction catalogue is normally only released 3 to 4 weeks beforehand. Within this time you need to conduct all the research, have a mortgage ready, speak to solicitors, research the property and get the required surveys.

If you can't or don't pay the balance you will lose the property - and you could be sued for the difference if the property eventually sells for a lesser price.

This creates a lot of upfront expenses, as not doing the preparation is a foolish risk, but then if you don't win the property you are out of pocket. The property is offered as is and once you win the property the responsibility is yours so you must insure it from that day and if there are any further defects discovered you will have no legal recourse against the seller or auction house.

There are two options of what to do with a property after purchasing at auction:

1. **Flipping it**, where you quickly renovate sell and move on to the next property

2. **Renovating it** to a good standard in order to put on the rental market and expand your property portfolio.

If you are planning to rent, look into the market while you're researching before the auction. When renovating, ensure that the work meets the need of the market.

Potential Strategy: ☐ Yes ☐ No

16. Vulnerable People

✠✠✠ £ £ £ ❺❾ 📖 ⚭

Especially suitable for those who enjoy working with different groups of society, don't mind being called at 1am in the morning and have access to a large number of properties.

These groups could include single mothers, disadvantaged teenagers, rehabilitation of ex-offenders, or recovering drug addicts.

Typically the rent is much higher than the average rental in the area – and amounts of up to £100 per night are not uncommon.

But this does come at a price and the price could be damage to your property, anti-social behaviour (even in the case of social workers being direct liaison with the tenants) and in the case of charities, even though the lease may have been for a long period, sometimes due to government cutbacks, the rental amounts may be reduced rapidly.

I once assumed a portfolio where some properties were rented to a charity where the rent per month was £1,150. With two months' notice, this was reduced to £550!

But the strategy can work if you are in the right sector, have the right house and are in the right location.

Potential Strategy: ☐ Yes ☐ No

17. Development

✠ ✠ ✠ £ £ £ ❶❷ 📖 🔑

This strategy is where we build properties or develop existing properties into other units in order to sell them off.

The rewards can be immense providing that you, as with any strategy, start small and work your way up.

The easiest way to start with development is houses into flats.

You've probably often seen those large Victorian houses that have been converted into 3-6 flats or even nowadays small terraces that have been converted into 2 flats.

This is the bread and butter development that a beginner to development should start with.

It allows you to purchase a small unit, add massive value and walk away with a profit (if you do your due diligence and get your numbers right).

There have not been many books written on this subject but a good place to start would be with Mark Brinkley's excellent book The House Builders Bible. Early on he tells us:

Never forget that property developing ... is a very risky business... You are assumed to be a sophisticated investor; make sure that you are.

My top tips for succeeding in this area are:

1) **Do your calculations correctly right at the start.** Note down every single item because any contractor will charge for separate items. If you're going to install a new bathroom, make sure you note down the detail such as:
Remove old bathroom suite and dispose
Remove old flooring and dispose
Paint ceilings with bathroom paint
Replace light fitting with new three bar bayonet fitting
Make good walls, fill in cracks, plaster where appropriate and paint walls with bathroom paint
Sand down door and skirting
Paint door and skirting with white gloss
Refit new bathroom suite and dispose of packaging
Scree flooring, use boarding where appropriate, lay down new lino
Reseal windows

2) **Always add on contingency and overruns.** With the exception of a few projects that I've done, most have overrun. They can overrun on budget but they can also overrun on time.
Have a feeling for how long a job will take. When you are getting quotes ask them to specify approximately how long each job will take. This will allow you to plan in a rough project guide

that should allow you to manage it (if you do manage it, see below).

Whatever quote you get; add on at least 10%-15%. It's to protect you and it's also to ensure that you do have additional money in the pot should something go wrong.

Sometimes *you don't know what the wiring or the plumbing or the internal structures are like* until you start pulling walls down.

Sometimes boilers do fail. Sometimes you need to put in an RSJ (a big lump of steel) when you thought you had a support wall only to find it's not.

3) **Take on board a professional project manager**. A project manager is worth his weight in gold. If you find the right one they will manage contractors and the project for you, and be your first point of call as to what is going on with the build.

Typical costs vary but allow 5%-10% of the build to employ somebody or alternatively use someone on a day rate (but be aware you won't get the same quality of service as they won't respond to calls or contractor issues if they are not ON the job on that day).

Get recommendations from local architects or investors as to who they use and get at least 2-3 references from them on jobs they have managed in the past.

4) **Don't do the first development aiming to make huge amounts of profit**. If you make profit, then that's great but you need to treat the first one as a learning experience and aim to make a margin of 10%-20%. You should be making much more than this but the experience you will learn from the first one will set you up for the future.

5) **Consider doing some of the work yourself if you are good with your hands**. Not everybody is good at DIY but if you are somebody that is genuinely good and I mean being honest with yourself, then basic items such as painting or flooring or small scale plumbing may be items that you can do yourself to save costs.

   Just be aware that you should figure in an hourly or daily rate for yourself otherwise you will end up paying yourself nothing!

6) **Have a partner to help you**. Developments can be tricky business. If you can, then work with a partner who has different skills to you. For instance, if you are more hands on you may want to work with somebody that is good at figures and projects or finding finance to help fund your developments.

7) **Make sure your solicitor knows what he's doing.** Time and time again, I run into people that have started developing then run into issues with covenants or other problems that have curtailed or even stopped the development.

I used to work with a guy some time ago who was doing a multi-million pound development (and he had already done several of these so he knew what he was doing) and for some reason, their solicitor had not checked out some extremely restrictive covenants that prohibited them from building over one floor. That can be a problem when you're building a three-storey block of flats. It didn't end well for my friend and he lost an enormous amount of money.

So I put this in there to warn you and to make sure you ask the right questions – *are there any covenants that I should be aware of?*

With developments; try and do something that works for you and that adds value to the building you are converting.

Then move onto a larger development of maybe brownfield conversion or a larger unit, such as a club.

Potential Strategy: ☐ Yes ☐ No

18. Land

✠✠ £ £ £ ❶❷ 📖 🕯

This strategy is where you acquire land with the intention of adding value through gaining planning permission and building or selling on.

A land asset has uniqueness to it. We're not making any more of it and thus because of this, its value and its potential has become inflated and led to inflated house prices now commonplace in the UK.

Fred Harrison, a leading UK economist, put it best with the argument that land has no intrinsic value or adds to anything due to its disassociation from the value of houses and rent. It doesn't resonate any more today than it did when he wrote his best-selling book Boom Bust, The Depression of 2012 as nothing has really changed.

Banking land will always have value if you have deep pockets and are prepared to hold on to it. For most of us, land is just another thing that we'd like to have but can't.

There are opportunities through and lets discuss them further.

Land always has the potential to build on - providing we have planning permission.

Land with planning can go for £1,000,000 an acre; without, for as little £6-10,000. The difference is mind-blowing yet this is where the landowner makes his money and also where you should be able to see the reason why house prices have shot up because of this direct correlation with the value of land versus what nowadays developers are building on it.

Gone are the days when you see 2, 3 or 4 bedroom detached houses evenly spread across a new development. Today it's a block of flats here, rows of townhouses there which may still have 3-5 bedrooms in but only one parking space for a family of 4 to 6 people.

It's because of this high land value that developers have to build the developments they build to recoup their costs.

But let's look at it from the point of view of how we can generate income from this.

Say we were to source a piece of land without planning and go through the planning system. This is where we can generate income.

Look at brownfield sites, existing but derelict or vacant builds, and some areas of so-called 'greenbelt' land which are not, but you are led to believe they are. They are the infill spots or the land at the side of a village or in a village that hasn't been used for years for anything worthwhile.

The planning game can be a long one, and your planning gains are made when you purchase the land in the first place - not before you gain planning

But the rewards can be plentiful and especially considering that you could sell the land off to another developer to actually do the hard work, the rewards can be justified.

Consider linking this strategy with lease options, something that many land bankers such as the large developers have done for years. You will still need to put down sizeable deposits to do this but in some cases you may be able to do a joint venture (JV) with the owner if you have the know-how and they have the land.

Land has many opportunities- it's about looking at it as a potential development. Is it maybe a house, or a block of flats?

Common developments in years gone by involved corner plots and joining up of neighbours gardens. Planning regulations have been relaxed slightly so that town centre offices can now be converted so all of these opportunities lead to more opportunities for us.

Potential Strategy: ☐ Yes ☐ No

19. Buying Freeholds / Ground Rent

 £ £ ❺❾ 📖 ⚗

This strategy is about purchasing ground rents in order to control the freehold of properties.

A strategy I was introduced to many years ago by a good developer friend of mine, this is all about controlling freeholds.

In the UK as well as much of continental Europe, a lot of flats are generally leasehold. What this means is that somebody owns the land upon which it is built (the freehold) and they collect a small amount of money every year for the ground rent.

This is completely different to service charges, which involve many aspects such as maintenance, utilities and gardening.

This is to all intents and purposes free money for owning the rights to the land upon which a building was built upon.

I looked at a few the other day and here are some examples:

Example One

Ground Rent for Sale: £5,500.

Ground rent received: £500 x 1 unit

Term: 118 years.

ROI: 972.7%

Your payback is within 11 years.

Example Two

Ground Rent for Sale: £10,000.

Ground rent received: £300 x 10 units

Term: 115 years.

ROI: 3,350%

Your payback is within 3.5 years.

For those that wish to enjoy more of a passive investment, then ground rents and controlling freeholds may be one for you.

Potential Strategy: ☐ Yes ☐ No

20. Lease Extensions

⚔ ⚔ £ £ ➎➒ 📖 ⚱

This strategy focuses upon extending the leases on flats/houses which have less than 20 years left on their leases in order to sell on.

A lot of flats and also houses in London have leases that can be anything from 99 years through to 125 years.

A lot of these do come around to expiry and one strategy which can generate good profits is by focusing upon this very niche market of looking at how you can extend leases once you've bought a property.

A property that comes on the market with a lease of say less than 60 years will sell for substantially less than a property that has a 99-year lease.

Typically this is because a 99-year leasehold unit will be equivocally valued around the same level as a freehold unit.

However once the lease drops below 60 years, it will be valued at approximately 60% of the freehold value or against the number of years left; 30 years left roughly equates to 30% of the freehold value.

In this strategy, we'd be aiming to take over properties with less than 20 years leases left on them and then renegotiate the lease with the freeholder to extend the term.

Costs of this vary according to the lease remaining but as an example, a 60 year lease renegotiation could cost as much as £20,000 but then if the value of properties was £200,000 and you could buy it for £120,000, then it would still be worth doing.

Once we've negotiated the lease, we can then look to sell this on or perhaps to refinance (as often leasehold units with low tenure left will not enjoy the same loan to value as a stronger much longer leasehold unit).

Potential Strategy: ☐ Yes ☐ No

21. Title splits

⚔⚔ £ £ ❶❷ 📖 ⚱

This is where you split a house into flats, then split the title so they are individual FLATS, then re-mortgage to get the value back out.

It's particular relevant in the case of somebody already owning a house where the rental yields have dipped.

For instance, in Northampton rental yields on 2-3 beds are 5% or 6% so there is an opportunity to split the unit.

A 3-bed terrace will sell for around £100,000, but a 2-bed flat will not go for any less than £75,000. Creating 2 one or two bedroom flats from a unit may increase both your capital value and rentability as average rents would be around £400 per month versus £600 for a 3-bed terrace.

How we do this is by ascertaining demand for flats in the area and bringing in an architect to look at the viability of creating flats from the property. Typically you'd be looking at two flats although if you added in basement and attic conversions, this could rise to three or four if some of these were studio units.

Once we have gained the planning permission and started to essentially create the new units from the existing units, we move on to the next phase - splitting titles, which generally goes hand in hand with refinancing.

In the case where we've converted the attic and basement we could potentially gain four units giving the following financials:

2 x 2-bed flats valued at £75,000
1 x 1-bed flat valued at £60,000
1 x studio flat valued at £50,000
Total: £260,000
Old Value: £100,000.
Cost of works: £60,000.
Profit: £100,000 (if selling on).

Rental Yields
3-bed terrace £595 pcm
2-bed flat £450 pcm x 2 = £900 pcm
1-bed flat £350 pcm
Studio £300 pcm
Total new rental value: £1550 pcm

Be aware…
- Only do this when the clear profit can be demonstrated even if everything goes wrong and valuations drop by 10%.

- It's critical you have exit options to get out of this. Don't start converting without an exit strategy to either refinance and spit the units as this may impact upon your mortgage and your ability to sell in the future.

Potential Strategy: ☐ Yes ☐ No

22. Flat Conversions

⚔ ⚔ £ £ £ ❶❷ 📖 🗝

__Tie in the refurbishment strategy with a focus upon flat conversions and you can create a tidy profitable business.__

A clear focus on converting properties into flats can yield great returns if planned out carefully.

This strategy ties in nicely with the refurbishment strategy but is a specific niche where the focus is upon adding value through conversion of units into flats.

A 3-bed terrace in Northampton will sell for £80,000-£120,000 but a flat will sell for a minimum of £60,000. To convert a 3-bed terrace into three flats would yield at least £180,000 in value. Conversion costs would be around £35,000, meaning a profit of £70,000 or more.

This can work particularly well on larger buildings such as disused clubs and pubs where the square footage verses the cost price are often disproportional.

A pub recently sold in Northampton for £115,000 which was the width of three terraces and could easily have been six to eight flats.

Potential Strategy: ☐ Yes ☐ No

23. Commercial

✠ ✠ ✠ £ £ £ 🔟 📖 🔖

This strategy is focused upon the purchase of commercial buildings such as shops, warehouses, offices and retails units.

Venturing into commercial was at first outside the scope of this book as I had envisaged most people wanting to get started in residential but then I got thinking that actually some of my more advanced strategies are very commercial in nature so hence why I've added this one in.

Again, this strategy is another one that has become very popular very quickly nowadays especially given the planning restrictions on converting offices to residential being temporarily lifted to allow for more accommodation to be built.

There are so many commercial opportunities out there – it's difficult to pinpoint one to recommend.

The key things to understand from commercial property are the following:

- The money is made in purchasing of a vacant building and then finding the long term lease that will generate the income.
- Rates are payable when they are empty.

- Inner city office rents are at an all-time low (but then many landlords do nothing to entice you to take them either. Opportunity?).
- Revaluation and refinance by adding value and adding in long term tenants is where you can pull out cash to reinvest.
- You can have multiple uses of a building - for example, a building with two retail units with offices above and warehouse out the back will have four to six tenants depending upon the split of tenants.
- The tenant is responsible for the upkeep and maintenance on the building. There's a first...
- Conversion opportunities do exist to convert an office into a residential usage but do ensure you still consult with planning and building regulations – a high profile "guru" in the west midlands recently had a warehouse of 70+ units condemned and was forced to turn the commercial property back into its original usage!

Potential Strategy: ☐ Yes ☐ No

Day #9: Service Strategies

This chapter is for you if you want to get into the property market but don't have enough funds yet.

These strategies can be started on a shoestring and help you develop a solid business model which, over time, should enable you to start buying properties.

Some of these options are full-time businesses, while others can be run part-time alongside existing commitments.

You will still need to put in the time and effort to make these ventures work and it is not any different from starting another business.

But – if you are serious about getting into property and right now, your access to funds is limited; these strategies can start to put a steady stream of income into your pocket.

24. Deal Sourcing UK

⚔ £ ❸ 📖

Set up an operation to source UK property.

If you want to build up a cash pot quickly, this is an ideal place to start. In this strategy, you source properties and sell on to investors or to a sourcing club.

You'll be finding these deals through estate agents, other lead providers and your own marketing.

You'll typically charge 1%-2% of purchase price for a deal. That means on a £100,000 property, you'll be taking fees of £1,000-£2,000. The keys to making this successful are:

a) **Dominating your area** so that you are the go-to person for property deals. Think niche, don't spread your wings across the UK. Instead focus on a very small tight patch

b) **Building up a database of investors** with cash who are ready to buy.

c) **Having a solid pipeline of leads to convert**. The more leads, the more deals you will sell.

d) **Having a system that works**. Consistency equals results and results equal income. Make sure whichever system you are following is reinforced by a system allowing you to maximise your time and minimise your admin.

Potential Strategy: ☐ Yes ☐ No

25. Letting Agent

⚔ ⚔ £ ❸ 📖 ⚲

This strategy is focused upon managing and finding tenants for other property owners in a geographical area or online.

A rental property is a lease contract between the landlord (lessor) and the tenant (lessee).

A lease is the legally binding contract between the landlord and tenant outlining the rental payments and the terms and conditions.

This is a bread and butter business which many investors try but many people fail at. A lot of landlords fall into the trap of setting up a letting business to manage their own stock but don't operate as a fully-functioning lettings business.

Get started because you want to offer a service to other landlords. If that means managing your own stock, too, that's all well and good. But don't get into it because you think you have enough units so you should set one up. You'd be better setting up a portfolio management company instead.

Still want to get started in lettings? Think:

a) **Management income**. This is your residual income that you will want to bring in so that you know that provided the rents come in, you are guaranteed to receive £X next month from the stock that you manage.

b) **Systems**. A really good lettings business will be driven by a system. People and sales are crucial but without a system you will end up spending 50% or more of your time on admin which massively impacts your ability to generate more business

c) **Pipeline**. A lot of agents leave this very important piece to the last and end up scrabbling around trying to find new instructions. It is as important to have new stock coming on as it is letting existing stock. Remember this and you will begin to develop a business that other agents will want to buy.

Fees charged would be anything from 6-10% for managing single lets, and 10-14% for multi-lets.

You'd typically charge £100 per let up to one month's rent depending on your area. There are another 27 different ways of generating income in lettings.

Through the way in which I teach people how to start and run a lettings business, you could be earning £10,000 net income within 12 months – if you take massive action.

You can get more details at http://tinyurl.com/mm-lettings

Potential Strategy: ☐ Yes ☐ No

26. EPC provider and gas certificates
✠ £ ➌ 📖

Energy Performance Certificates are required by the government before marketing whenever a property is built, sold, or rented. Gas certificates are required by law in all rental properties where a gas supply is present.

The Gas certificate requirement is enshrined in the Gas Safety (installation and use) Regulations 1998. This requirement requires all gas appliances in a rental property are checked annually, with a gas safety record being completed and a copy being provided to tenants.

An EPC contains information regarding a property's energy use and typical energy costs, they also include recommendations about how to reduce energy use and save money. To get an EPC you have to get an accredited provider to provide a certificate for you, see here for providers https://www.epcregister.com/searchAssessor.html.

Certain buildings do not require an EPC:

- Places of worship
- Temporary buildings that will be used for less than 2 years
- Standalone buildings with total useful floor space of less than 50 square metres

- Industrial sites, workshops and non-residential agricultural buildings that don't use a lot of energy
- Some buildings due for demolition
- Holiday accommodation that's rented out for less than 4 months a year or is let under a licence to occupy
- Listed buildings
- Residential buildings intended to be used less than 4 months a year

You can become trained as an EPC provider quite quickly and start generating income from £30-50 per EPC that you carry out.

Becoming a gas registered plumber is clearly much more comprehensive with a lot more work involved but there is a huge requirement for gas certificates with over 2.8 million rental properties in the market place.

Potential Strategy: ☐ Yes ☐ No

27. Bridger

⚔ ⚔ £ £ £ £ ❻ 📖 ⚱

This is a strategy for those with cash who wish to lend this out on UK property to investors and generate income on their cash.

This strategy works well for somebody that has funds available but does not wish to directly invest in the property market.

Most of the bridgers I know just lend monies and have very little interest in building a portfolio. There are exceptions to this rule of course.

So how does this work?

Essentially we take our funds and we lend them out for a percentage. We may also charge a set-up fee and we may also charge an exit fee.

So on a bridging loan application for a £100,000 property, we may decide that we will lend up to 75% so our maximum lending is £75,000.

We may charge an upfront fee of £1,500 to cover our legal costs and time to date. We may also charge 1% of the loan per month and estimating that this particular bridge is for 3 months, this would come to £2,250 fees. We'd also charge an exit fee of say £1,000 to exit the bridge.

Every bridger is different so these are just examples to bear in mind.

In this example, on lending £75,000 we'd charge £4,750 for a three-month period. That's a 6.3% gain - or annualised at 28.1%.

A much better return than the banks!

The strategy definitely works but you need to ensure that you have the right solicitors on board and that your money is protected.

Potential Strategy: ☐ Yes ☐ No

28. Software

✠✠ £ ❸ 📖

This strategy is particular suited for an experienced programmer and is where someone develops software for the property market.

Perhaps you can program and create applications that may be of use to the industry. From letting agents to EPC providers, there is software covering inventories, floor plans and property details, and helping with property management and bookkeeping.

Equally many can be improved and adapted. And there is plenty of room for innovation through applications.

For instance, could software be created that aggregated your leads into a calling mechanism connected to your phone to call out automatically without having to plug in the numbers? Corporate versions exist which are very expensive - but what about for the property investor?

Could a piece of software be created that pulls together all of the portals and lead sites into one software that allows you to look at the whole of the market in one glance?

Think of where you can add value to a process that already exists or think up how a new piece of software could solve a problem.

Potential Strategy: ☐ Yes ☐ No

29. Apps

⌘⌘ £ ❸ 🕮

This strategy is where someone focuses on developing apps for the property market.

Nowadays, you're being left behind if you haven't got a smartphone and whether you're an Apple or Android aficionado, the number of "apps" that have been created for them is astounding.

You can get apps for inventories, for receipts, for communication, for productivity - anything you can think of.

There are so many possibilities that exist for new apps to be developed.

Have a think about where you could add value to a service or product or area that already exists but is somewhat lacking in application support that could solve people's problems or help them become more efficient.

Potential Strategy: ☐ Yes ☐ No

30. Mortgage Broker

⚔ ⚔ £ ❻ 📖 ⚱

A mortgage broker acts as an intermediary who brokers loans on behalf of individuals or businesses.

Their role is to make property purchase easier by guiding the buyer through the range of mortgages on offer and finding the best deal for their circumstances.

Mortgage brokers have specialist knowledge of the property market, and provide financial advice. There are 3 types of mortgage broker:

1. **Those tied to specific lenders or just one, meaning they are tied to recommend their specific mortgages**. These brokers normally charge a commission on the mortgage rather than an upfront fee

2. **Those recommending from a 'panel' or selection representing a limited part of the entire market**. They can still purport to be 'whole market' brokers as long as their selection is representative of the whole market.

3. **Independent brokers free of tie**. They are in a better position to offer genuinely impartial advice although they usually charge a flat free upfront.

Being a mortgage broker is a role for somebody who wants to be in the property market but may wish to build up a sizeable pot of cash in order to invest into the market.

You will need to take exams in order to practice but these can be funded through working at a mortgage brokers or estate agency.

As you can see from above, there are many different types and you may wish to consider which one would work for you.

A mortgage broker is there to advise people on how much they can borrow. Then once your client has found a property you will need to then brokerage a mortgage and help them to purchase the property.

You need to be somebody that is interested in detail and finances as a lot of what you will be doing is going into detail with people.

Typically, you will be assessing financial circumstances in order to establish how much your client can borrow.

You will enquire about credit history, income, outgoings, and have to dig through a pile of documents to prove your client's financial position. You need to be prepared to dig through payslips, bank statements, P60s, utility bills, passports and more.

Following this investigation, you will be able to advise what repayments they can afford, the best interest rate (fixed or variable) and help get the best deal. You'll guide them through the lender application and following credit checks, you'll instruct a valuer to value the property. The lender then gives you a mortgage offer to pass onto your client.

Fees earned vary according to the type of mortgage placed but procurement fees are paid from flat fees through to a percentage of the sale. You can also charge for your services depending on what you are offering as a package to your clients.

If you were placing four mortgages a month at £100,000, you may earn £500 per mortgage giving you income of £2,000 per month.

Potential Strategy: ☐ Yes ☐ No

31. Insurance Broker

An Insurance Broker acts an intermediary between their clients and insurance companies.

They use their in-depth knowledge of risks and the insurance market to find and arrange suitable insurance policies and arrange cover.

This is a service that landlords need as properties have to be insured.

Again as with the mortgage broker, this is one area in which you will need to pass exams and often an insurance broker does other things such as mortgages and financial advice.

Potential Strategy: ☐ Yes ☐ No

32. Estate Agency

✠ ✠ £ £ ❻ 📖 ⚲

An estate agent arranges the selling, renting or management of properties and other buildings.

The role involves valuing properties including looking at the property condition and comparing with others in the area to get the best price for the client. They also market the property and negotiate deals on behalf of their clients. Estate agents often have to liaise with banks, building societies, mortgage brokers, surveyors, solicitors and other estate agencies during transactions.

This is an ideal role for somebody who likes the wheeler-dealer element of property but wishes to set themselves up to deal with both investors and residential buyers.

Building up an estate agency that caters to both groups allows you to be first in line to receive deals which you can then buy yourself or farm out to your investors.

Often a good estate agency will offer a lettings service as well to cater for investors on your books.

A typical agency fee for selling a property is 1-2% of the selling price so by selling two properties per month, you could generate income of £1,000-£2,000 per month.

Potential Strategy: ☐ Yes ☐ No

33. Furniture Provider

 £ ❸ 📖

A furniture provider sets up a company to supply furniture to landlords, setting up the property ready for the tenant to move in.

There are different options here. Student properties need durable, hardwearing, cost-effective and easy-to-clean furniture, Professional tenants demand a higher quality of furniture. It needs to be modern and solid, and with the extra cost incurred and care taken by the tenant it will invariably last a lot longer.

There are dozens of ways in which you can supply furniture to landlords, mostly for HMOs, show properties or social housing. Most single lets are let unfurnished.

An example of how cost effective this would be is in an example I often give at HMO seminars.

The normal way most landlords furnish a house is by going to Ikea or Argos.

Get a good cordless drill, hammer, screwdrivers, knife and your old clothes on. Take kettle & food. Spent approximately 40 hours to put together furniture for a six box house – and this is using furniture you've made before and are familiar with.

Order pizza and collapse into bed vowing never to do it again

Approximate cost £3,654-£4,228

Or what a smart landlord will do is order a furniture packaged from a reputable supplier (www.hmofurniturepackages.com for example).

Have it delivered and installed by a team of installers with all rubbish removed. Have your house ready in less than 24 hours.

Approximate costs £3,899 to £4,499

The cost differentiation is so minute that it seriously is not worth doing it all yourself.

It is therefore possible to set up either a local or national operation to supply landlords with furniture for their properties.

Potential Strategy: ☐ Yes ☐ No

34. Deal sourcing overseas

⚔ ⚔ £ £ ➌ 📖 ⚲

This strategy is focused upon sourcing but overseas.

If you want to build up a cash pot very quickly, then this is an ideal place to start.

In this strategy, you will be sourcing properties overseas which you can then sell on to other investors or through a larger sourcing company that has more investors on their books than you.

Typically, you'll be finding these deals through developers, estate agents, other lead providers and your own marketing.

You'll typically be charging around 1-2% of the purchase price for a deal. On a £100,000 property, you'll be looking to charge £1,000-£2,000 for a deal.

In some cases overseas developers will pay you commission up to 10% of the property value so you could possibly earn more than this but this is deal dependent.

The key with making this a successful business are:

    a) **Dominating your area** so that you are the go-to person for property deals in your area. Don't spread your wings across the world – focus on one or two markets maximum.

b) **Building up a database of investors** who have cash or are ready to invest. There is little point having the deals without the buyers.
c) **Having a solid pipeline of leads to convert**. It's truly a numbers game so the more leads you have coming in, the more deals you will do.
d) **Visiting your deals and locations**. You need to be the expert and have visited the country that you are promoting to ensure you understand what it is you are selling and that it is a deal that works and that your investors will come back again.
e) **Having a system that works**. Consistency equals results and results equals income so make sure that whatever system you are following you have a system in place that allows you to maximise your time ad minimise your administration.

Potential Strategy: ☐ Yes ☐ No

35. Utilities

 £ ❸ 📖

Being a utility broker or provider which will include gas, electric, telephone and broadband services is another way of generating income.

In single lets, the tenant takes over the accounts and place them in their own name; payment is usually a matter between the tenant and the utility company.

However in HMOs this is included in the rent meaning that the landlord is normally responsible.

You can therefore set yourself up a broker or introducer for the various utility companies around that will pay you for new clients. There are none that I recommend; however I know several people making significant incomes from utility service introductions.

I'd recommend you do your due diligence and understand the market you are getting into before you move into this market but you will typically be earning a small percentage of the bill every month plus an introductory commission.

This could be £20 for introducing a new client plus 0.5% of their monthly bill. That doesn't sound very much but the critical element with this business is numbers talk – so the more you have, the more you will earn.

Potential Strategy: ☐ Yes ☐ No

36. Negotiator

⚔ ⚔ £ ❸ 📖

A negotiator specializes in mediating agreements between parties.

They work to negotiate property deals between purchasers and sellers, trying to compromise with both parties to reach a happy medium and get the best deal available for both parties.

In property this role is often taken by estate agents negotiating with sellers as to what their property is worth, and the perspective buyers getting them to match this price, and as a result pay commission.

This particular strategy is well suited for somebody who excels at speaking to people and negotiating deals.

I've seen negotiators charge anything from £30 to £100 for initial negotiation then a success fee based on level of discount from sale ranging from fixed fees to a percentage of the sale.

If talking is your game, then maybe setting yourself up as a freelance negotiator may be the way to go.

You may need to start by offering services for free in order to get some testimonials but if you have the gift of the gab, then you should be able to build up a nice little business negotiating deals on behalf of clients.

Potential Strategy: ☐ Yes ☐ No

37. Inventories

 £ ❸ 📖

All single let properties and even HMOs need a good quality inventory so if there are issues later with damage to the property, this can be relied upon in court or via the deposit schemes to back up the landlord's claims.

Becoming an inventory clerk is a role which is suitable for those people who are detailed orientated and want to work within an environment where they are collating information, taking pictures and producing reports for their landlord clients.

There are many different applications and tools helping you carry out this task effectively. With more than 2.4 million letting transactions per year, there are plenty of opportunities to make money.

By focusing on a local market place, you should be able to build up a good income by providing this service to landlords and also agents.

Potential Strategy: ☐ Yes ☐ No

38. Information Publishing

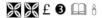 £ ❸ 📖 🏋

This strategy is all about providing information to people who are looking for how-to guides.

There is a lot of information out there and a lot of people looking for information.

It is certainly possible to start up an information publishing business to take advantage of this insatiable demand for more product, more information and more knowledge.

In recent years, we've seen a new monthly magazine start, countless different information products created and a whole set of new experts appear on the scene. But nobody seems to be really focusing on the information publishing side of the business.

I myself have digital products that sell from £7.00 through to £2,497.00 as well as physical products that sell from £8.00 through £997.00.

For the creative and content-minded entrepreneur, there is an opportunity out there to monetize this market in a very real way.

Potential Strategy: ☐ Yes ☐ No

Day 10: Ultra Advanced Strategies

39. Fractionals

❋❋❋££££❶❷📖🕯☎

This strategy is particularly suited for properties in a area popular for holidays and is where a property is sold in intervals - commonly 1/8 or 1/16 shares.

Several unconnected buyers can safely combine their resources to collectively own a property. This innovative way to purchase provides complete legal and tax benefits of property ownership passed through to you, or your heirs, and may be sold at any time.

Not to be confused with timeshare options, in a Fractional ownership you actually own a slice of the property. When you sell you have a physical asset to market, which gives you the realistic opportunity of making profit.

In a timeshare you pay for the right to stay in 'your' property for periods of time over the year; which isn't exactly attractive when trying to sell. Fractional ownership provides reassurance with a smaller initial outlay for a property you're likely to only use for a maximum of one month a year.

As you are only buying a part-share of the property, you can afford to purchase a more lavish and opulent property than you could fund outright.

For investors looking to spread their funds into as many different properties and markets as possible, as well as for those seeking a luxury home-away-from home, this is the perfect option.

Fractional ownership is a great opportunity for developers wishing to expand their reach and move into more lucrative markets.

The typical fees made on selling a £2 million pound property as a fractional would often end up with individual 1/16 fractions selling for maybe £250,000 each. That's £4 million revenue - but every deal is different.

As part of my travel and leisure background, I was very much involved with fractional ownership and this works particularly well on large estates or manor houses where the opportunity to add in services such as restaurant, leisure club and bar make a huge difference to just selling a part ownership in a house.

But this can work in many ways, particularly in holiday destinations. Say somebody wants a holiday home in Cornwall where prices continue to rise. A 4 bedroom house could cost as much as £500,000 outright. If this was divided into eighth-shares and people bought each for £100,000, this would generate an additional £300,000 in income.

Potential Strategy: ☐ Yes ☐ No

40. Care Homes

✠✠✠ £ £ £ ➎➒ 📖 ⚲ ☎

This strategy is particularly suitable for those who have experience in HMOs, social housing, and development, or those wishing to generate additional cash through buying a care home.

There are barriers to entry:

- Typically a care home would not sell for less than £500,000. You would need commercial finance on this and for those without a track record or experience, this is difficult to secure.

- You need to pass exams and be accepted as a care home provider of accommodation.

- You will be looking to generate income of £400-500 per week from every bed in your care home so the yields can be huge.

- Management is also critical in terms of ensuring that the appropriate systems, checks and balances are in place to management the care home appropriately.

Another way into the care home market is to develop your own smaller care home and then sell this on or lease it out to a care home provider. This is growing!

Potential Strategy: ☐ Yes ☐ No

41. Resorts

✠✠✠ £ £ £ £ ➎➒ 📖 ⚲ ☎

This strategy is ultra-advanced, requires large amounts of capital but can make you a fortune provided you buy in the right location.

Resorts are literally groups of holiday lets/apartments grouped together with additional facilities such as private golf courses, swimming pools, or private beaches.

Investing in a resort at a basic level would involve purchasing a hotel room. The types of resorts available would be part of an international marketing network that ensures significant occupancy, whilst the hotels facilities help achieve the significant room rates.

These two factors can lead to very high net incomes on hotel resort schemes, and whilst often more expensive to purchase than business or budget hotel rooms, can achieve 8 to 15% net yields.

Investing in resort hotel rooms offers the investor the best of both worlds with income and capital growth, as well as the opportunity to enjoy the property for a period of each year (dependent upon each scheme).

For those investors looking for personal usage and visiting the same location every year, resort hotel room investments could be the ideal solution.

Strategy for investing in resort property involves choosing a location with strong demand from a solid and growing target market, which could be a popular tourist destination, but always research supply and demand and choose the right property in the right location and with a reliable exit strategy in mind.

When purchasing a resort hotel room or property before the resort is running, the off-plan period could be two to five years due to the large scale development required for a fully integrated resort with excellent facilities. This means the investor benefits from early purchase discounts but doesn't receive income for the off-plan period. Weigh up this verses buying into an existing resort but with a lower discount.

The other way is to purchase a resort and do this yourself. It will cost from £3,000,000 for a small resort but the rewards can be significant, with six-figure net incomes per year.

This isn't for the faint hearted - but for anyone with any hospitality or operations background it's one that could work well if you can acquire a resort that is in distress.

I'm working on such a project at the moment. It's a 96-unit, £5.5m project with a £1.5m annual turnover. Through appropriate systems management and marketing we could increase turnover by £500,000 and reduce costs by around £200,000-£300,000 per year.

Potential Strategy: ☐ Yes ☐ No

42. Super HMO (Houses of Multiple Occupancy)

✄ ✄ ✄ £ £ £ £ ➎➒ 📖 🕯 ☎

A super HMO is what I call 10+ bedrooms. This is similar to the HMO strategy but on a big scale.

Think boutique, think luxury, think different and go out there and see what is available to purchase.

One we did recently in Northampton was a 14-bed luxury boutique HMO where en suite units are rented at £550 pcm. This delivers profits of around £2,000 per calendar month.

You can do this with old office buildings, clubs, pubs and warehouses.

But don't try to rent the property out as you would a six-bed HMO. You need to have something slightly different in there in order to stand out from the crowd and also attract at least 10 tenants into the same house.

Potential Strategy: ☐ Yes ☐ No

43. Super LHA (Local Housing Allowance)

⚔ ⚔ ⚔ £ £ £ ❺❾ 📖 ⚗ ☎

This is a multiple LHA bed strategy in one house – i.e. you could rent out a 4 bed 2 reception rooms to 3 LHA tenants on 1 bed rates.

With the changes in the LHA rates, it is becoming more difficult to get decent returns from LHA.

But there are ways in which you can increase the amount of rent from LHA tenants through looking at a house not as say rooms but as flats.

So a 4-bed, two receptions house could be let out to six tenants at £59 per week as a HMO, but you'd probably need to pay the bills.

Or you could rent out a bedroom plus another room as a lounge and this would be classified as a self-contained flat. This would jump up your LHA rate to around £85 per week.

Now clearly £85 x 3 = £255 per week, versus £354 per week on the HMO rate. But there would be no bills to pay. You'd bring people in to the house and between the three of them they'd need to pay the bills. As they are LHA, there would be no housing benefit payable. But they would need to pay for the utilities.

It's less hassle for some landlords and in some areas of the country it works really well as the LHA rate is £100+ per week thus giving excellent returns.

I've seen it used very well in the north where a £50K property could be receiving income of £100 x 2 per week from two LHA tenants.

You will need to become very proficient at LHA regulation and law and need to explain what you are doing to the council but it's a very good way of generating additional income from properties that aren't generating the returns you need at the moment.

Potential Strategy: ☐ Yes ☐ No

Day 11: My Journey

I've been involved in property and business for a long time now and I wouldn't give up the freedom or joy that I get when I see my clients or students succeed for anything.

Let me tell how I got to where I am now.

You see, I wasn't always living the life of my dreams; there was a time when I was working for major European and American corporations that sucked out every ounce of your energy

But that's not the start of the story; that's somewhere in the middle.

The early beginnings and college
My early beginnings began back in the East Ridings of Yorkshire in a place called Kingston-Upon-Hull. Much maligned by many who have never been to it; it's a city that has to make its local economy work because it is really the only major city within 50 miles of anywhere that has the ability to provide employment, infrastructure, entertainment and amenities to its burgeoning population of workers and a growing student market.

Life for me was growing up in a middle-class type of family where my father was a policeman and my mother a mixture of clerical, sales, receptionist and looking after everybody else roles. Most Yorkshire people are understated, often misunderstood and don't always expect much from life about from get some qualifications, get a job, then leave 30 years later and enjoy retirement.

The old adage "its grim up north" always brings a wry smile to my face because its both true and false at the same time. It's the same kind of statement that all unemployed people are bums living off the state. It's the few that it applies to – not the many.

For my part spending my formative years growing up in Yorkshire; most people are hard-working and wish to better themselves if they can. But who is there to teach them?

The government – no, they just want to keep you in the worker-bee mentality.

The schools – no, they just implement government policy and have you heard of many "entrepreneurial" schools?

The local business support organizations – no, they are more interested in either generating subscriptions or meeting their government imposed quote for contacts than helping people break free.

So, how did I become the businessman I am today?

Firstly, because nothing much was expected from me, I was determined to succeed and because of that I gained good enough grades to allow me to go to Oxford to study Theology.

For those that aren't familiar with Theology, it's the study of religion, the bible, doctrine, philosophy, ethics etc. Its not the most common path to becoming a businessman but back then my goal was to become a priest.

As I experienced the wider world and came into contact with things I'd never experienced in Yorkshire, the reality of whether I really wanted to become a priest or not became more and more apparent to me and in the end, whilst I was offered a parish assistant role in Bedford that would have led to me becoming ordained, I ultimately decided on another path.

I'd been involved in various business ventures along the way including a yard sale at the age of 8 that my mother quickly shut down (!), Young Enterprise where we set up a business selling promotional items to our fellow students, a European Society who raised money to support events and at college, I was employed by the conference office on a variety of roles; one of which was selling college merchandise to the visiting European summer students.

It was an interesting exercise for me to understand how people bought goods based on promotions, word of mouth and referrals. I actually made my best set of sales by selling in bulk to a student who was either getting them for his family or selling them on. It didn't matter too much as for me it was the experience of being involved in commerce that lit me up to want to get more involved in the business world.

Working Life to Leaving

From college, I would up working as an Trainee Business Analyst at Europcar – the car hire firm at their head office in Bushey, Watford. I remember that I won the place from 600 applicants that they had received and it wasn't long before my entrepreneurial skills kicked in and I had worked out various ways of making my role more efficient so I could spend more time on the internet researching different ways of making money and also suggesting new ways in which we could do things that made sense to me if not to my manager at the time. However, I did learn quite quickly which departments actually made the decisions and which departments were "support" departments. My department was in charge of Pricing and Revenue Management (essentially the art of extracting more money from a sale based on supply and demand) and it was clear to me that this was the lynch pin in the organization in order to generate the most amount of cash for the company.

Needless to say, change was at work and within 18 months of being a "trainee", I was heading up the department after suggesting to my boss that he apply for a role at another company paying £10,000 that he was earning at the time. He applied, he got it, I got his job. It probably helped that we'd had 3 other trainee analysts in the space of 6 months (one of whom was one of my best friends) who had all been and gone within 3-6 weeks of being employed to other better paying jobs in the city!

I figured out that it was a good strategy to ingratiate myself into the senior echelons of management wherever possible and through some astute steps managed to talk myself and another manager into the weekly board meeting. Being able to listen in and then share our opinions on the pricing, revenue and forecasts of the company proved very useful and illuminating for me and helped prove my worth to the board.

However, I forget to mention an important point that very shortly into my tenure at Europcar, I got married and moved 67.5 miles away. Now doing a 135 commute every day isn't everybody's cup of tea but I did do this for nearly 4 years but was getting to the stage where I was literally getting up at 6am and getting back at 730-8pm every day – sometimes driving half-falling asleep because I hadn't got enough sleep the night before.

The crux for me to move on came when a new marketing director was put in charge and I'd organized for 100 Mercedes A-Class cars to be moved to Blenhiem Palace for a 3 day international finance conference. The exact figures escape me but we generated something like £25,000 profit from that one deal and I remember him having a go at me because I was out of the office for three hours sorting it out.

I found new job a few months later and it was ironic that my board courted me for three days to stay with them including offering me a lot more money, a better car and better working conditions. I was touched that the Managing Director said I was family but in the end, I turned them down as I had been making noises for some time and I didn't really see how the overall culture was going to change that much for me to continue to make a difference. Maybe if I stayed, I'd be the MD now ☺ ...

The new job was 10 miles down the road for a major international corporation based out of Indianapolis, USA called RCI – the leading provider of timeshare exchange in the world.

I was brought into manage European pricing and landed headfirst into a company that was already going through its own change having recently being bought out from its founder and sold to a major American conglomerate called Cendant. Based on my looking-in on the political situation, when an opportunity came up to head up and manage a European Business Management Initiative, I jumped at the change and organized a worldwide emergency conference in the UK for about 40 staff to kickstart the European recovery of our business.

SIDE NOTE –as you get involved more and more in business, you'll get to understand a lot about shareholder value. Personally because of where I am right now, I completely get it but I don't really like it very much. The European business I was in at the time was making MILLIONS but because of aggressive completely unrealistic targets, it was not behind budget and thus deemed to be failing ... I wonder sometimes

Anyway, probably because of the maverick side of me and the position I was in, I wrote a paper about how we could REALLY turn around the business and go to the next level and sent it to the MD. To say I had an interesting , volatile and forthright chat with my boss shortly after was an understatement to say the least J

Anyway, to cut things short else I'll carry on writing for sometime and that should really be in a book 20 years from now; due to the catalysm, I became Head of Revenue Management for EMEA (Europe, Middle East and Africa) with a department of 11 spread over four locations and built up revenues across several products line by $20 million over a 3 year period.

I enjoyed for some an enviable life of creating products, spearheading growth, negotiating huge contracts and travelling the world. But the hours were long, the pressures were immense and the stress sometimes overcoming. Sometimes you wouldn't really know where you were as it was just another hotel room and let me tell you that whether its in New York, Cancun, Munich or Orlando – a hotel room is a hotel room.

It was here though that I really found out about politics and how this can damage a company and damage a person's reputation and future prospects. I'd become more disenchanted with the organizational tendencies to essentially cull a large amount of staff every December because essentially this balances the balance sheet and allows you to improve your on-paper performance (as the redundancy payments don't then hit until the next financial year if you time it right) and the internal politics that everyday I had become embroiled in because of my departments central pivotal role in the business.

It's also interesting how a person can make or break a career and I had been very lucky to date working with some great bosses and bosses of bosses to make my mark. After having reported into the Chief Operations Officer and the Chief Executive Officer at RCI, it was when I was handed back to a new Chief Marketing Officer that things began to untangle. People who know me well will know that I don't suffer fools gladly, I don't do people who speak bull, and the fake laugh brigade are not on my Christmas list. This new guy was all of the above and worse, he had the most awful over the top fake orange tan you've ever seen and he thought he was a charmer with the women...

It was truly awful and within the space of 30 seconds, I knew we were going to have trouble

I won't go into details but let's say within 18 months of him joining, I left of mutual accord with a payment for my troubles. I sometimes wish I had a tape recording of some of those conversations I had – it would have been interested reviewing the trite I had to put up with many years later.

I remember clearly giving my leaving speech in our department (knowing that there were about to become even more redundancies) and saying, when you don't feel the passion anymore, it's time to move on.

And for me, it was well past time.

Property Investing

I got seriously started with my property business back in 2003 (whilst I was still at RCI) but have been involved with property in both my career and as a participant since 1993. I had always been interested in the dynamics and opportunities that capital appreciation could make but never really understood just how powerful an asset class property was until 2003.

It was on yet another trip to America when I was stood in the Staples store in JFK Airport browsing the business books (even then I had a keen interest on bettering myself anyway I could) when I spotted a strange lurid coloured bright book called "Rich Dad Poor Dad" by Robert Kiyosaki. I started reading the first chapter and was hooked. I devoured it on the flight and immediately spoke to a good friend and colleague at work when I got back about the concepts I had been exposed too. Needless to say "Mind Your Own Business" or MYOB as we shortened it too became our favourite phrase and still is today.

We took a one day course with an American called Chris Szabo. The day was interesting because it talked about more than just property but businesses, investments and property. It really helped to open up our eyes and help us to understand how some of the concepts Kiyosaki talks about in his book come together.

Further encounters were not as promising and at one event where Dolf De Roos was meant to attend, he never showed. However, this is where I met the charismatic Sunil Jaiswal who went onto become my mentor and at the event described how it was possibly to double, triple or even quadruple the amount of money you could make from just one property.

This was of course through Houses of Multiple Occupation (HMO's for short) where a property is rented out by the room to young professionals, students or key workers. After many hours of reading, a few more low-cost events and lots of research, I decided to bite the bullet and invest £3,500 into a 2-day residential workshop in Milton Keynes.

The weekend changed my life for ever. I remember thinking halfway through the day that it isn't what you don't know, it's what you don't even know to ask about things that you thought could be impossible.

But as my mentor said "**_impossible is only an opinion_**" and how true he was.

I went on from that course to build up a £3.5 million pound property portfolio which was gained in just over 18 months through trial, tribulation, sweat, tears, blood, stressful times, tenacity and sheer dogged passion to succeed. There is no magic pill but in live events, I share some of my strategies to achieve the goals I set myself.

Through the this time period, I was picking up a house every 2-3 months or so, then moving onto the next one and it was a completely crazy time with the market being on the up, solicitors being able to work within creative boundaries and the banks bending backwards over themselves to lend you money.

It wasn't all plain sailing though and I probably lost out on c £6-8 million pounds worth of deals through not acting quickly enough, brokers messing up, solicitors being dilatory and vendors and sales agents disappearing. But throughout this journey, I was driven to succeed through the support of my colleagues, my mentors and my family.

However, what I found is that once I had my portfolio; I had essentially done what Kiyosaki warns will happen and I had essentially become a Self-Employed person. I didn't really have a business per se that could be operated without me or had systems and processes in place to allow me to hand over responsibilities to another person. I had become a victim of my own success and I know from speaking to a lot of business and property owners that many of you will identify with this.

I then undertook a process that took me the best part of 2.5 years to create an operational platform upon which I could essentially handover control (if I wanted) to another person to run my business for me, I spent hours on creating systems and processes that were fool-proof and essentially created a McProperty empire which to this date takes me less than a few hours per week to keep on top off (in fact probably less than one hour).

Once I had invested my time and energy into this, I emerged with a sustainable business model that ensured my financial security whilst allowing me to replicate what I had done.

Subsequent to establishing my portfolio, my base and my financial security, I then dabbled in various areas including a networking group, a sourcing company for UK and USA properties, a packaged furniture company, various online ventures and more things than I care to mention.

Through all of this, I realised that actually I knew a hell of a lot more than I thought I did and this was probably through working on and in my businesses with over 24,940 hours to date of direct experience that I believe that I could help people who had been in my position to build up their own profitable portfolios and allow business owners to escape from their businesses through setting up processes and marketing systems that work for you and not control you.

I was encouraged to share my experiences with others and did my first talk back in 2006 at an event in Milton Keynes and from then started to talk at various events around the country sharing stages with Parmdeep Vadesha, Vanish Patel, Rhett Lewis, Glenn Armstrong, Ranjan Bhatacharya, Simon Zutshi, Jim Halliburton, John Lee, Juswant Rai, Anthony Lyons and more.

I developed the first and still the largest HMO authority site in the UK www.yourhmoexpert.com which even today receives over 2,000 visitors a month even though of late in the last few years, I have been very remiss at keeping it updated. (But that all changes this year). This website gives tons of free information, advice, articles, video logs and audios that you can read, listen and watch to make you a better investor.

It was when I was on the main speaking circuit speaking at events up and down the country that I then met the two guys who would become my business partners in a new venture; Millennia Property. The idea around this was simple – based on my operational and marketing experience and my brand exposure coupled with sales and financial experience, we would build a new company that educated people, built portfolios and grew a national chain of lettings offices.

Unfortunately this was just as the major slump hit and we were unable to secure the right type of funding so we ended up growing the business organically.

Within 18 months, we had over 500 units under management in five offices (Northampton, Leeds, Colchester, Lincoln and Hemel Hempstead), we had educated over 600 investors across the UK, we had taken over £16.5 million pounds worth of stock on instalment contracts, lease options and delayed exchanges and we had completed building projects worth £1.8 million in Northampton.

It was all heading in the right direction but it just wasn't to be. We had disagreements about the go-forward, the way the business was run and the accountability of directors, so I had to make the very painful decision to consciously break up this company and go back to the drawing board.

Many lessons were learned and it's an experience that I will always remember but for now, that was the past and now is the future.

Moving On and Where Am I Going With All Of This?!

I am on a lot of forums, groups and email lists and I often hear people spout lyrically about how you can learn everything you need to know on a forum and you don't need to spend any money on courses. In my opinion, its utter nonsense and either these people have already spent thousands on poor courses and felt ripped off or they have 1, 2 or 0 properties and shouldn't be somebody you take a lot of advice from anyway.

I consider myself successful, I consider myself financially free yet I still pay thousands every year to mentors, coaches, home study courses and to attend workshops so that I may learn more and better myself.

I guess it's a way of living and for me, I relish the interaction, shared learning experiences and access that you cannot get via a digital online medium.

I wholeheartedly believe that when the student is ready, the teacher will appear – and for some of you, the time may be now for you have this book in your hands.

For others, you may need more time or need somebody different that you resonate more with.

For me, its all about giving enormous value and I take great care to ensure that I am working with like-minded people who will follow the advice I give them and take action against it.

Its about

RESULTS

Its about

PURPOSE

Its about

ACTION

As of today, I run the following businesses:

Wealth Success Alliance – the go-to exclusive club for high net worth individuals and business owners who want to make even more money, play even more and have even more fun! We reinvigorate your business so you can enjoy it more.

Our motto is basically: financial security equals lifelong happiness.

Let's see how we can help you.

We effectively offer two services:

Done for you – we help cash-rich time-poor new and existing investors access the highly lucrative world of HMO's and build a million pound portfolio hands-free over a three year period. Very exciting and highly demanded with Discovery Days every month to learn how this works.

Done with you – we help both cash-rich and cash-poor new and existing investors who want to explore property get the appropriate correct training and coaching to help them achieve their goals. We're gaining accreditation right now with national government bodies and landlord organisations and are already a partner of Shawbrook Bank and Endsleigh Insurance.

Stanford Knights Letting – a bespoke letting and management agency that manages properties across Northamptonshire, Cambridgeshire, north Bedfordshire, Manchster, Derby and soon other areas in the country.

We manage everything from studios through to large executive houses. We specialise in houseshares and can advise on the necessary regulations required to make your house safe.

We charge reasonable but not cheap fees. We deliver great value and are there for you to make your business successful for you.

HMO Furniture Packages –a national firm that works with landlord to furnish any particular type of property from studio flats right through to boutique hotels.

Our focus is upon quality furniture at reasonable prices that lasts.

Often Misunderstood

Sometimes people fail to "get" my humor and my methods. Maybe some personal background will help.

Guitar, Music, The Great Outdoors, Family

I'm a big time music fanatic. Since secondary school I've been listening to the likes of Bryan Adams, The Beatles, Bon Jovi, The Mavericks, Diana Krall, The Travelling Wilburys, Kate Rusby, The Bushburys, to name a few.

I'm a guitarist and singer-songwriter. Yes, I've been playing guitar since the age of 16 and learnt to play in the long summer after my GCSE's whilst I was waiting to start my A-Levels. I've been writing songs for over 22 years and I love playing and singing.

I've played in bands, been recorded, and even shared the stage with luminaries such as Waterson Carthy, Martin Simpson and The Paperboys. I currently am active on my local music scene and gig 1-2 times a month in a variety of bars, clubs, hotels and at the summer festivals!

I love the outdoors and have walked many of our great long distance footpaths including The Cleveland Way,

Coast to Coast and the Pennine Way (at least most of it as north of the English border has always alluded me on this walk). I enjoy nothing more than an invigorating stroll around my local area and although I yearn for the hills of Yorkshire, its possible to find a few nice walks in the southern counties (Sywell, Oxfordshire Downs, Exmoor to name a few come to mind). I also relish reliving our history and exploring old houses and castles – the work of organizations such as English Heritage and National Trust is second to none and if you've never been to one of their places, you should put it on your list to do this year!

My humour has always leant toward sarcasm to the point of being serious, and has been used all my life to weed out a few good friends from among 6 billion other people of Earth.

Favourite movies are the ones where revenge and vigilante justice is doled out by unlikely heroes coupled with classic sci-fi and fantasy movies and action movies – roll Maverick, Jack Bauer and Frodo Baggins into one and I'm made up.

I have two gorgeous children, Callum (13) and Amelia (9) who are the light of my life and keep me on my toes. Home for me is somewhere in Northamptonshire although the hills of Yorkshire will forever call me (unless a nice boutique villa comes up in the French Riviera or New England).

I am a big big fan of travelling and exploring new places. Key highlights for me are the Americas, continental Europe and the Carribean (although a trip to the Indian Ocean before it disappears is high on my agenda). I like to find those little places that are just off the beaten trail so whether it's a local bars in Madrid serving 5 bottles of Corona for 3 euros (yes 3 euros – isn't it crazy) or a idyllic quiet little park in Cancun 2 minutes from the strip or a martini and cigar bar in downtown Indaniapolis; I'm for it.

Food and drink play a big part in my life and I am a keen fan of the finer wines and cooking a la carte whenever I can.

Where Next
To summarise this all to a point then that completes the circle of truth and the journey.

When I first got started in the property industry, my big **REASON WHY** was to leave the corporate culture and do something for myself.

Because I was earning a good salary I had to replace it quickly and my first focus was **HMO's** (Strategy One). Once I left my job (18 months later), I looked at other strategies and it does take some time to find the right one that fits with your particular skillset and interests.

I tried **BTL** (not really for me; the returns just did not justify the effort), I ran a **SOURCING** company for a while (UK and International) but the client liaison took up too much of my time and I was part of a **UTILITIES** network marketing team but whilst the residuals were good; it took too much time away from my core focus.

I then happened upon **LETTINGS** where today a lot of my focus is as I found that I understood the model, could make it work and it dovetailed nicely with my portfolio.

I've moved more into the **INFORMATION PUBLISHING** business nowadays but I am fairly unique having HMO's, lettings businesses and an Education and Mentoring business.

I spend less than 10% of my time on my HMO portfolio, 20% of my time on my lettings business and 70% of my time on my education/investment business.

This is slightly different to my core recommendations but this is down to leverage which we will discuss later on in the book.

Day 12: Review and Preparation.

This concludes the strategy section.

We now need to review where we are. Today's all about reflection and making some personal decisions on a go-forward plan.

We'll then move onto the main bulk of the book which is all about getting your property business set-up and running by the end of our 30 days together.

What Level of Investor would you say that you are?

Investor Type	Tick This Box!
Beginner	
Intermediate	
Advanced	

Beginner - if you are just starting off, then this is a sound one for you to progress.

Intermediate - if you already have some properties or have been working in the property industry for 3 years plus

Advanced - if you have more than 10 properties or have been actively investing for 5 years plus

What amount of funds do you have?

Funds Available	Tick This Box!
Low	
Medium	
High	
Ultra High	

Low - £1,000 to £10,000

Medium - £10,000 to £50,000

High - £50,000 to £199,000

Ultra High - £200,000

What payback timing are you aiming for?

Payback Time	Tick This Box!
3 Months	
6 Months	
12 Months	

3 months - for speedy returns

6 months - for quick returns

12 months - for medium-term returns

59 months - for longer-term returns

60 months or more - for pension planning

What level of education do you have?

Education Level	Tick This Box!
Blue	
Red	
Indigo	

Blue - you should be fine with reading at least three books on the topic, attending at least one networking event in the first twelve months and being on at least one property forum to ask questions.

Red - you should in addition to Blue ensure that you attend at least 1-2 full day workshops on your chosen subject plus seek out a mastermind group for intermediate to advanced learning. A coach would also help accelerate your knowledge.

Indigo - in addition to Blue and Red, it is imperative that you have a mentor and are part of an on-going coaching and mastermind group in order to support your journey and your plan.

Do you feel that there one or two strategies which resonated with you at a higher level?

If you've answered yes – great. If you've answered no, then perhaps you should reread the strategies chapters in order to understand the different ways in which you can generate money from property.

Which business sector do you think you're going to focus in?

Beginner   Intermediate   Advanced
                    Services

As a personal barometer for yourself, what is your level of experience of starting a business?

Business Experience	Tick This Box!
Low	
Medium	
High	
Ultra High	

Low – I've never owned a business before.

Medium - I've worked in a start-up organisation before or I've been investing in property for one year or more.

High – I've started up at least one business of my own or I've been investing in property for five years or more.

Ultra High – I've started up at least three businesses of my own and either sold or closed these down or I've been investing in property for ten years or more.

Now we've answered these questions, it's now time to create or even recreate your business from scratch and start making it a successful, sustainable and profitable business.

Day 13: Choosing Your Strategy

How do you choose a strategy when there are so many to choose from?

We've talked about 45 strategies in this book alone - and there are variants upon variants being employed today.

But how do you choose the one or two that are right for you?

The first place to start is to ensure that you have a thorough understanding of your plan and financial goals.

Understand the parameters you have available in time, money and experience. And equally importantly, passion. If you're not remotely interested in a strategy then don't for heaven's sake commit to it and start putting time and effort and money in. It simply will not work.

Use these factors as a starting point to eliminate those strategies that don't work for you in terms of experience, time or money. Trust me; this will make sense to do it this way to begin with.

For now, remove from your list of choices the strategies requiring time or money you don't have. But remember - experience can always be learnt or bought, so don't disregard them entirely.

Hopefully you've not got a list of less than 10 strategies which may be suitable. Anymore, and I'd say that you have not been quite – ahem – honest with yourself.

Now complete the short following exercise in your workbook.

I want to have £_____,_____ coming into my bank account every

week/month/year by ___ / ___ / ___ .

I want to spend _____ hours per week on my property business.

I have £_____,_____to invest into property right now.

I have _____ people that I know of that may have £___,_____ to assist me on a JV basis to invest in property together.

From owning a property business, my outcome is to use this to enable me to

Now that you've completed this exercise, put your top 10 strategies (or a lesser number if that's what you're left with) into the table in your workbook and then work through the process steps required in order to determine which one to two of these strategies you should focus upon first.

Read this in line with your life plan and the points you added above.

Now you'll need to refer back to when you very first started this process and be completely honest about strategy and whether you can pull it off or not.

Focus first on funds required, payback time and kick off.

Education can be achieved very quickly. Others may take some time.

So if for instance you've identified that Auction is a strategy to consider - you're passionate about buying at auction and enjoy the thrill of bidding against others, you have the time to do it, the payback works and you have the money but you do not have any experience - this can still be a valid strategy for you.

But if you're interested in Care Homes but you've no experience, you want your payback in 12 months but you only have say £20,000 to invest, then this may not be the strategy for you right now.

Focusing Down on The Top Three Strategies For You

Now you've been through your list of the top ten strategies, there should be some clear winners in terms of those strategies that meet with your financial goals.

If you are not completely sure, then this is probably the time to really search your heart and reconnect with yourself in order to understand which strategies appeal.

There is no point in doing a strategy if you fundamentally do not agree with its ethos, it does not excite you, or you are only doing it for the money.

You need to live, breath, eat and sleep with this strategy in order to make a difference to your life.

So, take a deep breath and write down the top three strategies that you believe:

- Resonate with your inner core
- Will give you the lifestyle you want
- Allow you to get started within 30 days to start making money.

Write them down now:-

STRATEGY ONE

STRATEGY TWO

STRATEGY THREE

To start your property business or even if you are doing property right now and you are already doing one or more of these strategies, there has to be a core focus.

It's almost like doing a double honours degree. If you're studying say English language as your major, most of your time will be spent on this. If your minor is Classics, much less time will be spent on this.

I want you to focus on no more than two strategies - like you're working towards a double honours degree.

The second, or minor, strategy is one which can be on set and forget, and later benefit from the proceeds. Something which requires your on-going input is not going to work as a secondary strategy.

Here's an example:

If you choose HMOs as your first strategy and Sourcing as your second, I can guarantee that one of these will suffer because it's not possible to do both well in tandem.

However, if you choose HMOs as your first strategy with say Tenant Buyers as your second strategy then while there is work involved in the second strategy, you could easily buy two of these per year at the same time as focusing on your HMO strategy.

Remember it's the long game we are working to here. And there are different rules depending on where you are in the journey.

New To Property?

You need to select one strategy as your major strategy. This is where you are going to spend approximately 70% of your efforts.

The other will be your minor strategy. You're going to spend approximately 30% of your efforts on this.

Already In Property?

If you aren't already following any of these strategies, you have a predicament.

Either you need to extract yourself from the current strategies you are pursuing or you need to put this current strategy down as your minor strategy. You will still be following this strategy but not focusing the best part of your efforts on it.

Alternatively, ensure you have systemised this particular strategy to the point you're not actually spending more than 10% of your time on it each week. If you're not at this level you will have to put it down as your minor strategy.

MAKE YOUR CHOICE

You can change this at any time but for now, I want you to commit to a decision. Which two strategies will you follow?

Make that choice now.

MY MAJOR STRATEGY IS:

MY MINOR STRATEGY IS:

Brilliant! Now you've made a choice I'd like you to fill out the following page which is also included as a download.

I _____ [insert name]

Commit on _____ / _____ / _____

To creating my property business and graduating with honours in

[insert your major]

With *[insert your minor]*

I understand that the journey may not be easy. I understand that I will struggle. I understand that I cannot do it on my own. I realise that there may be times when I want to give up but **I will not**.

I will never give up because

I will persevere and overcome any obstacles, I will take care of myself and my family, I will leave a legacy for others, I will do good in the world, I will achieve my goals because by achieving them, I achieve my dreams. I will laugh, dance and be crazy.

Most of all I will create a property business that is profitable, sustainable and fun.

Signed

Day 14: A Life Without Vision Is A Life More Ordinary

You have now created a vision for your life, and it's time to chunk it down into categories that relate to your business.

You can also use this plan for your personal life. I'd highly encourage you to do so. For now, let's focus on your property business.

Let's say that you have a vision to have a property business generating £100,000 a year. This enables you to have four holidays annually, to drive a nice car and live in a nice house with a bolthole in France.

We need now to make it a reality. The only way to do this is to work backwards from your vision to where you are right now.

Here's an example to get you thinking along the right lines working back from your end outcome.

Year	Outcome
10	£100,000 per year from property and business portfolio. Holiday apartment in France 6 Multi-let and 18 Single Let Properties
5	£84,000 per year from property and business portfolio. Holiday apartment in France 5 Multi-let and 10 Single Let Properties
4	£67,200 per year from property and business portfolio. 4 Multi-let and 8 Single Let Properties
3	£50,400 per year from property and business portfolio. 3 Multi-let and 6 Single Let Properties
2	£33,600 per year from property and business portfolio. 2 Multi-let and 4 Single Let Properties
1	£16,800 per year from property and business portfolio. 1 Multi-Let and 2 Single Let Properties

Take the next section and write down your 10-year plan, working backwards from 10 years ahead so you remain entirely in the future. Understanding your dream has to remain in your thoughts as you do this will make it easier to commit to these outcomes year by year.

It doesn't matter if it's slightly out at this stage. It doesn't matter if you are not entirely sure what strategies to follow. What matters is that you commit to putting this down on paper so that we can then get into the next section.

And it doesn't matter if it's slightly woolly at this stage either. What matters is that you write something that gets you excited and enthused about your goals

Year	Outcome
10	
5	
4	
3	
2	
1	

Fabulous. Now we have your plan. What we're going to do next is break this down into manageable chunks. Take a break, and I'll see you tomorrow!

Stage #2 of the 5 Stage Blueprint

Create

STAGE #2 CREATE

Day 15: The Next 12 Months Are The Beginning of Your New Life

Music Suggestions: Classical, soundtracks, reflective songs.

Everything you see around you began in somebody's mind.

It may have been a dream, a vision; an idea so powerful it took over their every waking thought – but it was the beginning of the creation of something more than them.

Indeed luminaries such as Thomas Edison, Roger Bannister, Michael Jordan, Tiger Woods, Walt Disney all used the power of imagination to begin creating their businesses within their minds until they were so convinced of the viability of their creation that when it came to manifestation in the real world; whatever they had dream about became reality.

This is the same for any business you decide to build.

Here is a story about how I created a national letting agency within 12 months back in 2010.

In 2009 I had sat down and come up with my plan for 2010 which involved growing the lettings business I had to managing 150 units of stock. We were currently managing 30 units with just one part-time member of staff and 2010 was looming ahead.

By chance a meeting with an investor before Christmas to manage a 14 bedroom HMO fell flat due to the work involved but in January I received a call from the same gentleman who had 9 properties he wanted managing as he was fed up and couldn't cope any longer with the day-to-day management, rent collection and maintenance demands. I looked at the portfolio and could see how it could be set up to generate money for him and for me and this was the start of the journey.

What I saw was that this small portfolio of 9 properties was in fact around 44 units of stock in terms of rooms and apartments and that this could spearhead the growth of the lettings business. I visualised what this would look with another 10 of this size of portfolio under our belts which at one portfolio a month would come to around 440 units by the end of the year and suddenly I was excited.

What for me had been a fairly interesting year in terms of my plans became an extraordinary year in terms of the possibilities of where we could go with this.

My operational skills coupled with the financial acumen and sales ability of my partners led us to take over another 14 property portfolio (around 58 units) within the next 6 weeks whilst we then negotiated to open up a further two offices in other locations.

Within four months we had four offices in Northampton, Leeds, Lincoln and Hemel Hempstead (two owned through joint ventures) and had increased our stock control from 30 units to a huge 483 units! We'd increased operating staff from 2 to 8 and support staff from 1 to 5.

At the same time due to our focus on acquisition; we had taken over 4 portfolios (2 were 10+ and the remainder were less than 3 units each) and our equity in these units was around £1.5 million.

Then came September and the biggest deal of our lives was about to happen. We had got wind of a landlord who was looking to emigrate and through a mutual friend had arranged a meeting. The houses were top quality and all professional houseshares.

After a meeting at a plush hotel in London, we signed the deal and went out to celebrate in style. In just two hours we had accelerated our stock base by 117 units with a rent roll of £51,000 per month.

By the end of 2010, we were up to just under 600 units with a rent roll of £152,000 per month!

All of this from visualising and setting out my plan for the year and from beginning to create this entity within the most powerful instrument we all possess – the mind.

Now I don't share this to boast but rather I share it to illustrate what is possible when you completely commit to a path and follow it through.

Anybody can start a business but few decide to start a business that in itself is Extraordinary.

A business that transcends nations, race, colour and pocket – a business that caters to its clients, its team, its shareholders and aims for the pinnacle of excellence.

Why do so few try? Because it's really difficult to be the best of the best.

Most people will rush headlong into a business without really understanding what it is that they are in business to do. Most people will set up a business to fail from the beginning. Not really a good idea is it? Most people will set themselves up in a way that restricts their growth, their opportunities and their ability to manage their extraction going forward.

But you're not most people are you?

In the 100K Club we go through a Creation phase that allows my mentees to truly embrace their business plan and vision and make it into a reality – a business that can make an extraordinary difference to the world but also create an enviable lifestyle for you.

If you're reading this book, I'm hoping that you are one of the few that wants to

- Make a difference with your business
- Bring a new way of doing things to the market
- Shake things up a little bit
- Be different – be cheeky - be wowtastic
- Give something back to the world

To really do this in a way that makes people sit up and take notice is not easy but nor is it unsurmountable. At the same time, this is about getting the mechanics in place first – it's almost like creating a plan to succeed rather than having no plan and thus setting yourself up to fail.

Rather, this is about using the power of Creation to begin creating the business of your dreams.

Quick Win.

Think about what you want your business to look like, think about how you want your business to serve others, think about what your competitors do and what you can do differently- to make a difference to people's lives.

The 12x4 Plan

Now you're clearer on where you are going, you need to make a plan to carry you through the good times and the bad.

This all starts by chunking down your next 12 months into 1, 3, 6 and 12 month goals contributing to your overall outcomes.

It's what I like to call the 12x4 plan.

The reason why we have to put this down on paper is we're 80% more likely to achieve something we write down than if we do not.

What's important is the physical act of committing to paper. This exercise makes the goal and the plan that much achievable because it is written down in black and white.

Sometimes it may scare the hell out of you. Sometimes it may seem small. Sometimes it may confuse you. But more often than not; it will inspire you, it will motivate you and it will push you towards achieving this goal - the goal that you want more than anything.

And you do want it, right? Otherwise you'd be reading a book, watching TV or doing something else with your time that doesn't contribute towards you achieving the goal or dream that you want for yourself.

Let's take a look at Bill.

Bill doesn't have a lot of money to get going but has found a joint venture partner. He wants to purchase a distressed property, refurbish it to a high standard and sell it on to generate additional money for him to use as a deposit on a property for himself to buy at the end of the year.

His two strategies to begin with are Refurbishment and Buy-To-Sell.

Let's split this out in the 12x4 plan:

Month	Task	Outcome
1	Research market for appropriate properties. Make contact with estate agents and auction houses. Draw up joint venture contract. Research local builders and select three to quote based on prior work and typical prices. Find solicitor that can complete the sale.	Groundwork in place to move quickly.
3	View 100 properties per week (via online portals). Visit 10 properties per week in person. Make offers on 2-5 properties per week that meet requirements. Move forward on one property. Get quotes for refurbishment. Complete sale. Refurbish property.	Sourced property Refurbished property
6	Put property on market. Start researching properties that meet criteria for renting. Start viewing properties for second purchase	Sell property Pay back JV partner Research properties for next purchase
12	Purchase second property. Start refurbishment (if required)	Buy second property Refurbish if required

This plan is fairly simple and what I'd call a headline plan. What it does is clearly set out your outcomes so you have an overall aim you have to get to in order to tick off each box.

It's not yet broken down into months - but it doesn't need to be, because life can throw curveballs at you so the important thing is that we get a plan on paper that looks and feels like it could work. Next we go to work on actually its implementation in a way that helps us hit our targets at the four stages in the plan.

It's your turn. We'll divide it up into your two strategies so that you can start planning in right away how you are going to achieve your overall plan.

Strategy One		
Month	Task	Outcome
1		
3		
6		
12		

Strategy Two		
Month	Task	Outcome
1		
3		
6		
12		

Tomorrow we'll look at how we take this and ensure that you are focused on making this happen on a weekly and daily basis.

Day 16: Creating A World Class Planning System That Works

The R-P-A System

The whole ethos around how we plan needs to change.

We cannot plan using a to-do list. This just doesn't work. We just keep adding items and don't actually complete anything, or find the time to celebrate what it is that we have done. Our planning needs to be done using the R-P-A system. This is a system I've adapted from several of my mentors and is based on Tony Robbins RPM system.

The way the system works is as follows:

Results – what is the result that will be achieved through adding this task, project item or communication item to our R-P-A list?

Purpose – what is the purpose behind doing this particular task? Does it drive us nearer to our outcome or away? Does it resonate with us - and are we committed to it?

Action – will we take action on it? Will we take massive action on it? Will this task be acted upon and carried out?

Bear this in mind in terms of anything task that you capture and you will start to master the art of planning.

Your Hour of Power

Once we have the next 12 months planned out, you can put this into a weekly planning exercise.

My mentor Tony Robbins refers to this as your Hour of Power and it's so true. It's an hour where you truly focus on you, your vision and what you want your life to become.

If you skip this your week will generally turn into a week of reacting to other events, getting some of your to-do list done (if you've written them down) and wasting time on activities that are not moving towards your ultimate life and vision.

So how do you go about planning your week?

1) Ensure you have a plan and a vision for your life. If you don't, then no amount of weekly planning will allow you to progress to live the life that you want to live.

2) Your weekly planning session should take place either late on Friday before you jump into the weekend or on Sunday afternoon/evening in order to prepare for the week ahead.

- It's important you reconnect with the reasons why you want the outcomes you have planned for, and why they are important to you.

- You'll then need some form of planner. You can use an online planner or an off-line planner; either work well depending on what your attitude is to technology. But you will need some kind of system that allows you to block time out.

- At the very worst, use an electronic calendar on Outlook or Google.

- Put in any diary appointments you absolutely must attend for the next week. This should include personal and business appointments. It'll give you a sense of what is already scheduled that you cannot move (unless you choose to move them).

- Capture all of the key tasks and communication items you have to get done for the following week, and make a list of all of these.

Once you've done this list of tasks which will probably be between 80-100 individual items, you'll want to prioritise them.

Why do we do this?

Because the list will include some items that are crucial, and others that are nice to have.

Now you need to prioritise every task or communication item that you've listed. There are different ways you can do this, either by using numbers or letters.

You can rank them:

1 or A – Important and needs to be done in order to achieve my outcomes.

2 or B – Not Important and doesn't need to be done today in order to achieve my outcomes.

What we are aiming for here is a list of the 1s and 2s (or As and Bs) so when we come to planning our week and day, we are focusing on the tasks that absolutely need doing rather than working through a to-do list which does not work.

Now we have this list, it's time to focus on the top 3 priorities you have for each of your outcomes and plan in how they are going to happen throughout the next week by setting time aside for them.

These need to be appointments that you set with yourself but that you plan into your calendar so they actually take place. Most people set out the week with good intentions but do not actually ever end up completing most of their tasks. This is because they do not plan them in.

Here's an example of how this works.

Month	Task	Outcome
1	Research market for appropriate properties. Make contact with estate agents and auction houses. Draw up JV contract. Research local builders and select three to quote based on prior work and typical prices. Find solicitor that can complete the sale.	Groundwork in place to move quickly with Refurbishment strategy.

To get to this item being completed, there are probably a dozen or so actions that need doing.

You know what your outcome is from the planning you've already done so you know what you need to get achieved for Month 1.

So some typical actions you'd brainstorm may include:
- Finding three websites you can use to research local properties

- Sourcing 100 properties to review online
- Attending networking session in Bristol
- Requesting recommendations for a solicitor on property forums
- Asking for builder recommendations
- Find a JV contract that can be used for working with other investors
- Walk the streets and make contact with at least three estate agents
- Get a website domain name
- Get business cards produced
- Speak to Lenny about his refurbish project and visit to learn more
- Ring Cheryl about estate agent contact
- Narrow down selection to 10 properties to visit
- Get a property inspection report from the property forum
- Get literature from 3 banks for new account
- Speak with Business Link about accountants
- Create a flyer
- Find a printer to print the flyers
- Find someone to help you distribute the flyers

These need chunking into sections and then ranking. Here's an example of how this works.

Monday.
- Find three websites that you can use to research local properties
- Ask for recommendations for solicitor on the property forum

- Find 100 properties to review online
- Walk the streets and make contact with at least three estate agents
- Get a website domain name
- Get business cards produced
- Speak to Lenny about the building he is refurbishing right now and see if you can visit to learn what he's doing
- Get literature from 3 banks to decide which account to open
- Create a flyer

Now chunk these into similar activities.

Online Research (Properties)
<ul><li>Find three websites you can use to research local properties</li><li>Find 100 properties to review online</li></ul>

Town visits
<ul><li>Walk the streets in Bristol and make contact with at least three estate agents</li><li>Get literature from 3 banks to decide which account to open</li><li>Speak to Lenny about the building he is refurbishing right now and see if you can visit to learn what he is doing</li></ul>

Set-up Activities

	• Ask for recommendations for solicitor on the property forum • Get a website domain name

Marketing
• Design business card • Get business cards produced • Create a flyer

Now that you have these activates chunked into similar categories, you can now plan out your day along the following lines.

Time	Activity	Outcome

0900	Marketing
	  a) Design business card
	  b) Create flyer
	  c) Get business cards produced
		Professional appearance and literature to hand out

1000	Marketing	

1100	Phone Lenny
	
	Set-Up Activities
	  1. Solicitor recommendation
	  2. Website domain name
		Get access to real-life project and understand how it is being put together
		Have solicitors to ring to put in place for sale.
		Have professional domain for clients to view.

1200	Lunch	

1300	Online Research Properties
	  1. Find 3 websites
	  2. Find 100 properties
		Have a list of properties that may be suitable for refurbishment

1400	Online Research Properties	

1500	Town Visits
	  1. Walk the streets in Bristol and make contact with at least three estate agents
	  2. Get literature from 3 banks to decide which account to open
		Make 3 new friends
		
		Have information on bank accounts

1600	Town Visits	

The key in the way you plan is by focusing upon the 1s or As that need to take place.

You can still schedule in the 2s or Bs but it's not so important to complete them.

A task that's been classified as a B may end up becoming a A because it becomes important, but often the B tasks end up falling off the task list because you understand that they do not carry you along to your overall outcome but are just peripheral activities that do not add a huge amount of value.

Daily Planning

The second aspect to your planning is carrying out a daily planning session.

This needs to take place ideally the night before so that you can review all of your activities and tasks for the day, look at what still needs completing and then schedule in the next day.

It is possible to do this first thing in the morning as well but you will waste 10-20 minutes if you do it on the day in question rather than the night before.

Firstly I need to get you to understand this important element of this planning system:

You do not carry on working until you have completed everything.

This is absolutely critical.

The reason we prioritise is to make sure we are aiming to get 100% of the A tasks completed. But this isn't to say that when we begin the process of becoming task-oriented we won't overestimate what we can get done, and end up only completing 70%-80% of our A tasks.

That's fine. Do not worry! It takes time to master this and unlearn your old habits.

To schedule in the following day, you need to:
- Review the tasks you completed today

- Move any A tasks you did not complete onto the following day's agenda/plan. This could involve rearranging your plan, which is fine - but be aware of this particularly if you are using a pen and paper system (you may wish to just block out your appointments at the start of the week then each day fill in the following day's appointments)
- Brainstorm any additional tasks that came out of today that you feel need noting down. Prioritize them as As and Bs.
- Commit to the following day's activities, then stop for the day.
- First thing in the morning, quickly check email (no more than five minutes) for anything urgent that came in overnight that you feel needs adding to your priorities for the day.
- **Go take massive action!**

This is a simplified version of how planning actually works and I am only basing this on your property business. It may be that you have another business, a job, you may have other personal categories that you need to fit in, you may have other goals that you want to achieve that are above and beyond what we can cover here.

But this should give you enough steps to get cracking. There are more advanced strategies that follow on from this that can accelerate your growth even faster but for now, this basic planning tool will put you ahead of 90% of your peers – that I can guarantee.

Now it's your turn

Commit to your hour of power.

I'm going to carry out my hour of power on:

Friday afternoon/evening

Sunday afternoon/evening

Let's capture some action items in your workbook.

Now let's capture a list of tasks (i.e.projects or things you need to do) for the following week:

Now let's capture a list of communications (i.e.email/phone) for the following week:

What calendar items do you already have in place for the following week?

Now let's chunk these into tasks which are similar to each other:

You can now use a planning tool such as a diary, online calendar (Outlook or Google Calendar), or a productivity tool to block book your calendar for the following weeks with your:

- Calendar items already booked (such as meetings and appointments)
- Chunked tasks that relate to each other
- Downtime (you cannot work all day, every day)

Now we've got a great planning tool under our belt, we can now go onto building our business. The next chapters really focus upon getting your business up and running as quickly as possible.

Take a rest – you've earned it today!

Day 17: Your Business - You Cannot Own Properties Without Owning A Business

The main difference between investors who achieve their dreams and those who loiter on the hard shoulder are their attitudes and commitments to business.

A lot of investors that I speak to don't separate property income from personal income in a way which is easy to manage.

Lots of people may have a separate personal bank account for their properties but it is my belief that for you, the reader of this book, that this will not be enough for you.

To be serious about property is to be serious about business. And this means setting up your property investments as a business - completely separate from your personal bank accounts.

You cannot run your properties as a hobby or a side-line. Do this and you will find that you will run into trouble later down the line.

You must treat your properties as a bona fide business and as such you will need to set yourself up as a business.

What kind of business can I run?

There are several different types of business that you can set up:

Sole Trader. This is where you operate on your own, generally as a separate business with separate business account. Essentially you operate as yourself with little protection from any potential litigation or debts if you are unfortunate to incur them later down the line.

Limited Liability Partnership. This is where you operate with one or more partners and your risk is limited to the amount of funds put into the company. Many solicitors work in this way so that they can add new partners as and when they come on board.

Limited Company. This is where you set up a separate entity which is limited typically by shares which you normally hold or if you are working with others, you can decide upon a share split and shareholders agreement correspondingly.

There are many ways to set up your property business but the most important thing is setting up your properties in a business you own.

The structure can be relevant from the beginning depending upon how you wish to run your business and potentially hand over your business but for most people, getting started down the sole trader route will probably suffice.

It's best to take advice from an accountant on this depending upon your tax position who can then advise you accordingly.

I can however point to recent Government legislation regarding Section 24 of the Finance Act 2016 which effectively will penalise property investors owning properties in their own name.

In short; this Act comes into force in April 2017 and through 2020 will taper away interest relief that you can claim on your mortgage.

Without going into the technicalities of the taxation, your individual circumstances and what this means for you as an investor; as a property expert with over 14 years of experience I will leave you with this.

Companies can claim the full 100% relief on any interest payments made on a mortgage for residential purposes.

Individuals will no longer be able to claim a tax-free allowance anymore and *most* investors will find them pushed into the higher tax brackets and end up *subsidising* their properties from profits which do not actually exist!

Some other thoughts to take away though on what may work:

1) Are you looking to run your business as a side-line and continue with another job or business at the same time?

   If you've answered yes to this question, then maybe a sole trader route would be best for you.

2) Are you looking to take partners into your business at any time in the future?

3) Do you wish to be liable only for the amount of money you put into the business?

   If you've answered yes to these two questions, maybe a limited liability partnership route would be best for you.

4) Do you wish to operate an entity that is separate from you that builds its own profit and loss, can have loans made against and to it, and can ultimately be sold if you so choose?

5) Do you have other businesses so don't necessarily want to take any profits out of this company at the moment?

6) Do you wish to pay yourself a low salary and then claim dividends at another time in order to improve your tax situation?

   If you've answered yes to these three questions, then maybe a limited company would be best for you.

What is your vision for your company?

A company lives or dies by the vision of its founder.

Similar to how we discussed how important it was to have your dream and vision for life, your company needs to have fire breathed into it so it will stand the test of time and become the company of your dreams.

Statistically most small businesses fail within the first 2-3 years of trading. Avoid being part of this statistic by focusing on the vision for taking your company out of your house and wherever you wish it to be.

A grand vision is easier to buy into than a small vision that doesn't get you excited in the morning when you get out of bed. Believe me: I've been there many times in the past and if you go down the route of working for yourself on your business, then you need this motivation in order to drive you onto the next level.

It's the motivation that will drive you when the going gets tough and you don't really feel like doing that next phone call, or writing that next letter or putting that web page up when all you really want to do is watch TV, have a cup of tea or surf aimlessly for no other reason than the fact that you don't have a compelling reason for doing what you are doing - and you are not bought into the vision that you need for your company to make it work.

So let's get this vision down right now by answering some of these questions?

1) What do you want your company to look like 5 years from now?

2) What changes do you wish to make with your company?

3) What culture do you want to have in your company?

4) What experience do you want clients to have with your company?

5) How do you see your company making a difference in your industry or the wider world?

6) What will you give back to your local, national or international community?

    These are just a few to be thinking about in order for you to create a compelling vision that your staff and you can buy into.

    I have a few different companies and it doesn't matter which one you are working on that day, you need to have that vision, that accountability and that motivation to drive you forward and make it work for you.

    Here's one of mine for Wealth Success Alliance:

Wealth Success Academy is <u>the</u> go-to exclusive club for high net worth individuals who want to make even more money, play even more and have even more fun!

We play to win, we play to give back and help others, we play so that others can benefit from our efforts, we play so that we can leave a legacy for the future.

Financial security equals lifelong happiness!

Set some time aside and come up with a vision that drives you forward.

Day 18: Property Business Basics Part 1

Most of us who get started in business do so in a faltering kind of 'make it up as we go along' ride.

While this can be fine, I'd recommend a much better approach is to plan out your business first by using the template I've included for you to download. Then you will stand a chance of actually getting your business moving in the right direction without potential roadblocks half way down the road!

Spend the time preparing and planning, then when you come to implementation you will find it so much more effective you'll wonder why you didn't in the past.

There's a reason why athletes spend years preparing for the Olympics. There is a reason why a construction project delivered on time is project managed a year in advance, and there is a reason why an enormous ball is planned so that it pleases everyone who attends.

It's calling planning and preparation.

In this section I share some fundamentals to ensure you start off in the right way and also to consider things which you may not have thought of.

The old advertising slogan of Tesco - Every Little Helps - is indeed true when it comes to businesses. The general agreed rule of thumb indicates at least one third of new businesses fail in the first two years (Lacoma, 2012).

Business Account

This is the place to begin once you have decided which entity you will use to trade (sole trader, limited partnership or limited company). It's also possibly the one task that will take the longest to complete.

All of the major banks offer a business account facility but are they all up to scratch?

Some questions to ask yourself when opening up a business account include:

- Do I want somebody I can talk to who builds up knowledge of my business and can help me move forward in the future?
- Will I be handling lots of cash or mostly internet transactions?
- Do I want access to a large branch network?
- Will I be using online banking to carry out most of my transactions such as direct debits, standing orders, payments and more?
- Do I want free banking for 1 or 2 years?
- Do I want a debit card or a credit card?
- Do I want an overdraft?
- Do I want telephone support?
- Do I want a separate counter at the branch?

The accounts that are available for businesses vary in their service offerings, complexity and level of support. In my opinion having used all of the major banks over the last 10 years, none of then give you the perfect solution but all of them have something different to offer.

If you want the more personal touch, then I'd recommend a smaller bank such as The Co-operative Bank or Handelsbank.

If you want great online functionality I'd recommend HSBC, although NatWest is nipping at their heels.

If you use lots of cash, then all of them generally have two accounts - one aimed at the more cash-intensive business, the other aimed more at a traditional service type business.

Pros

A lot of the limited company formation organisations have links with the big banks and can get you appointments fairly swiftly (at least within a week) so you may wish to look at the different options available via the online formation companies as often they will also offer a cash incentive for opening the account through them.

Some of the trade organisations have specific bank accounts set up . One that comes to mind is the FSB account which The Co-operative Bank run. The benefits of the FSB account are extremely good compared with other offers but then this is probably because a bank has listened to an organisation with a lot of members who have listened to their members and got the best possible service from a bank.

Cons

Be aware the time to open an account will depend on how quickly you can get an appointment.

And even if you do get a relationship manager, banks tend to move them around like pawns on a chessboard and someone who you have built a relationship with may well move on.

Credit

How do you get credit with a bank?

You start by having a plan.

When you go to see the Business Account Manager or Specialist, they want to understand what your business will generate in turnover to match you with the right bank account. They also want to make sure you can get access to credit facilities if possible.

The industry that you say that you are in also influences what type and amount of credit will be offered to you.

Credit is offered following a soft credit search on your file being carried out so be aware if you have bad credit, you may be refused credit or even a bank account.

It is always better to ask for credit up front than to not ask at all.

Don't be shy of asking for a credit card to be put onto the account or a small overdraft.

Generally speaking most banks will give you some facilities from the beginning and this will normally be a credit card with a £500-1000 limit.

This is all you need to get started but the range can vary. I opened two businesses within 30 days of each other last year registered to the same address and I got a £1,000 limit credit card with one business and a £3,000 limit credit card with the other. The only difference was the SIC code (standard industrial classifications) which proves that the industry you are operating in does make a difference.

Trade cards

If you are in business, then you can get some amazing trade discounts provided you know where to go and who to ask for and where to shop around.

Most trade cards can be a combination of a credit facility (harder to get for new businesses) or a discount card which drops prices for the trade.

For the property market, here are some great ones to consider:

B&Q – TradePoint. This is B&Q's card for the trade. It has both a credit facility (up to 60 days) and a discount facility (special deals on trade items plus free or discounted delivery). You can use this at any B&Q and by swiping your card, you automatically get the discount plus where there is a separate TradePoint counter. You can get advice and guidance from the senior and experienced staff that can look for products and advise you on what is available to use. It's free to apply so if you will be using materials on refurbishment projects, then this is a must.

Staples Rewards/Staples Rewards Premier. Staples are one of the best sellers of good quality stationery and computer equipment in the UK. They also have a very good low-cost printing service. As I use Staples a lot for stationery supplies and printing, it makes sense to get a Business Card. Again, they have a credit facility (up to 60 days) and a reward card offering special offers and money-off vouchers. It's free to apply so if you are going to be doing a lot of printing and buying stationery, get a card.

Screwfix. Having a Screwfix account can help when you need items fast and B&Q do not have them. Typically getting around 30 days credit, you can order items up to your credit limit to be delivered next day or pick up in store in person. They do have a lot of items that B&Q don't stock so it's worth opening an account with them.

Jewsons/Grahams. The specialists for bathrooms and for general building materials are owned by the same firm. You can get a discount off their prices through NLA (see Trade Organisations) but you can also get a credit account with them directly or through intermediaries. Typical credit terms are 60 days and they deliver direct to site or you can pick up in person. I recommend these companies for larger scale refurbishment jobs.

Booker Wholesale. Although this chain is focused on the retail trade, it's worth getting a Booker Wholesale account. Normally Booker Wholesale is access only, and to get a credit account you have to build up business with them. They can be very useful for general shopping for bulk items and also they do have very good offers on year round on a variety of household goods. We generally use them for their cleaning products as buying in bulk gives us a better price over the supermarkets.

Regus Business World. If you are not starting out with an office a Regus Business World card is ideal to get access to their business lounges. They have more than 1,100 locations in 52 countries and a good amount of excellently sited locations across the UK. The benefits of joining include access to business lounges at any time, when you can use the internet, get free tea and coffee and also hire business facilities there if required. They are a great place to meet people and also to get work done if you are in the vicinity.

Loyalty cards

I include a mixture of ones that I use ALL the time and this is by no means the whole list and while I appreciate some people may think that this is trite, I would counter that by saying that it is not often that you get discounts or better deals through the normal routes to market. If you can get a slightly better deal or some points to use against something else, then why wouldn't you.

Most multi-millionaires did not get there by spending without checking out prices and offers first. Here's a selection of some of the good and not so good ones.

Wickes – My Wickes Card. This card gives you points against your purchases in Wickes. Essential if you are in there a lot as ultimately you can spend against the points and get special deals. But this card doesn't offer a particularly great reason to shop there.

Nectar. Once upon a time, this loyalty card was everywhere and even though they've scaled back somewhat, you can still get points in dozens of shops and especially at BP service stations where if you are going to fill up, you may as well get some rewards for it given the extortionate cost of petrol these days.

Subway. Like it or not, often business owners are running from one appointment to another. We can all nip through the drive-in at one of the major fast food chains but it's a sure way to an expanding waistline and higher cholesterol.

Subway have been maligned in the press for high salt content and this may certainly be true in some of their sandwiches but their low calorie (less than 350 calories) options taste superb and are much healthier than the alternative burger and fries. Get a loyalty card and get free sandwiches the more you buy.

Costa Coffee Club. Is it me or are they everywhere? Well yet again, you can get points for coffee (and cake) and these all add up to free coffee. And free shots. And more free things!

Shell V-Power. Shell runs their own loyalty scheme where you can collect points towards Air Miles or redeem them against your fuel bill. Well worth collecting.

IHG Priority Club Awards/ Club Carlson. There are a host of different hotel companies around and they all offer different loyalty programmes. If in the course of your business you have to stay at one then you may as well get some points and offers and discounts for doing so.

My favourites are the IHG Network including Crowne Plaza, Holiday Inn and Holiday Inn Express, and Club Carlson which has the Park Plaza and other brands.

You can also get a card nowadays for Best Western, Accor, Hilton, Premier Inn and so on. Shop around for who you use the most and start collecting points.

Tesco ClubCard. Most people have one, but did you know you often get better deals through Tesco Direct - and more points if you spend them there? If you are buying for your business, then make sure you are using your Clubcard.

McDonalds. Although not a loyalty card, McDonalds do some of the best-value tea and coffee around and if you're travelling, there is always one near you. Collect six stickers to get your next drink free. Given that many people drink a few hot drinks per day, it makes sense to collect the stickers. A colleague of mine once told me I was mad and I told him to just try it for a few weeks. I think I counted about 12 stickers posted on his steering wheel a few weeks later.

Stationery

A business should invest in some quality stationery.

This doesn't even need to be that expensive nowadays as both design and print of stationery can be extremely good value.

But why have stationery?

If you're a limited company, there are certain statures you have to adhere to and include on your stationery.

Secondly, having stationery says that you are an established business that people can rely on and will want to do business with.

Even though a lot of communication is done via email these days, people still want to see a bona fide company taking money from them.

Thirdly, having custom designed stationery is quicker and easier than setting up a template and hoping you have enough ink.

Having stationery printed with your brand, message and USP says a lot more about you than a Word document with ill-formatted header and address.

Where should you get your stationery from?

You'll probably need a logo designed first which shouldn't cost you more than £10 from a website like fiverr.com or get a local design artist (or student) to design this and the stationery for you which, if they are working off-peak (i.e. not in the studio but for themselves), shouldn't cost more than about £50.

Get your stationery as a first port of call from Staples or Vistaprint.

They will often do a business card, letterhead and compliment slip set for an all-in price.

When you're a more established and feeling comfortable about spending more money, use a local printer or printing.com franchise for luxurious paper and quality printing.

Office

To have an office or not is the question?

I firmly believe having a workspace to work from is very important but should you splash out on an office when you are just getting going?

My first answer would be no.

My second answer would be - it depends. If you are running a client-facing business where they need to come into your office, working out of your shed or home is not such a great idea.

But if you are running a business where you go out to meet clients, and then you can and probably should run it from your home to begin with.

When is the best time to get an office though?

When you are established, when you have good cashflow coming in and the pipeline has good solid prospects in, consider an office.

In terms of what type of office to go for, this depends on whether you wish to have premises that you are only in or wish to go down the serviced office approach.

Both can work well – both have their own little challenges.

Serviced Offices

Generally cheap and quick to get into.

You'll pay anything from £250 through £1,000 per calendar month for an office seating from two up to 10 people. That will generally include all your bills apart from telephone and internet.

You'll normally get desks, chairs and storage included.

The lease is generally on some kind of licence agreement where you pay one month's rent and one month's deposit up front for a 6 month to 12 month period.

Depending on the office, they will have a reception area, telephone answering services during office hours, a separate meeting room you can use and tea and coffee facilities.

There are serviced offices and there are serviced offices!

Some pretend to offer a range of services but do not so do your research carefully, view as many as you can and ask questions.

My preferred supplier is Regus. They may not be the cheapest but their product and service is second to none and you also get access to their business lounges worldwide.

Your Own Premises

You control what happens in your own place. You determine how you wish your offices to be portrayed. You decide how you wish to set out your offices and how you wish to interact with clients.

You're completely responsible for the upkeep, bills and running costs for your place. But it's all yours. And for some people that outweighs the costs of this verses a shared office environment.

And if you are in the retail environment such as lettings, estate agent or sales, then perhaps a street front presence might work for you?

The downsides are that it could take you 4-6 months (!) to get into your office as commercial agents and landlords are in my opinion (and experience) extremely slow.

Plan

Finally, you need to have a plan.

It's enough that you have managed to work your way down the myriad of different ways in which you might interact and work within a business, but it's now time to plan out your business.

Here are some questions to consider:

- What type of business do you want to run?
- What do you wish your office opening hours to be?
- How do you wish to interact with clients and suppliers?
- Do you want to meet people face to face?
- Do you wish to employ staff?

Write down the answers in your journal.

Day 19: Property Business Basics Part 2

I now want to focus on the next set of steps to get you up and running as quickly as possible.

There are some aspects of running a business where you will need to offer both the easiest way of payment for your client and also the easiest way for you to make payments.

There are also some essentials through which your business will not grow unless you invest in these both from a time and a money point of view.

Let's take a look:

Credit card payments

You will find no matter what business you are in that consumers love credit cards.

I doubt that we will ever get back to the days of saving up for something, then going out to the shop to buy it in cash. The ready-eddy instant culture is here and it's here to stay.

So what do you do when you are asked by your clients if they can pay via credit card? You have to say yes.

Here are some easy solutions to put in place for you to take card payments:

1) **PayPal**. The daddy of online payments (why do you think it's owned by eBay?). This will enable

you to take credit card payments on your site for goods that have a pre-determined price. PayPal process the payment, take their fee and send the remainder to your bank account within five days of your request. Essentially you can build up a balance in PayPal and decide when to transfer it, which may or may not be useful for you.

__Be very wary if you are going to take large payments all at once – we've had issues in the past and no longer use this facility. But for smaller regular payments; its fine.__

2) **Merchant account**. Often requiring a large set-up fee, of £150-£200, this allows you to take card payments of any amount - typically by a handheld machine. The benefit of this is that if you are in retail or training environment, you can tap the amount into the machine and take the payment there and then. The downside is terminals cost about £20-30 per month to rent and if you don't use them, then you won't get this back and it will start to cost you.

__We use Worldpay which is very good but there are many others you can use.__

3) **Card Readers**. There are several out there but the one I use is iZettle. Essentially a small card reader that slots into your iPad, iPhone or

Android phone, this allows you to take payments with the client entering their card PIN into an application on your phone which then processes the payment. Ingenious - and the fees are no worse than PayPal or merchant accounts. The beauty about this type of approach is they regularly run offers giving the card readers away for free. They are small and there is no running cost, so you just use it whenever you like.

Whichever solution you choose, choose one that works for you based on what you will be doing with your business.

Commercial / Business card

As part of the package that you should receive from your bank, one of the things that you'll need is a business credit card or charge card for your business expenses.

As well as maintaining a separate statement of your spending, it also allows you to manage cashflow more effectively as you will generally get between 30-45 days to pay the balance.

You will find with most business banks that they offer a credit card (where you can pay the lowest amount) or a charge card (which is effectively the same as a credit card but the full amount is paid every month). Whether it's Visa or MasterCard doesn't make very much difference in my experience.

Networking

There are a plethora of events out there for businesses.

There are networking groups such as BNI where you pay upfront membership fees and are then expected to be there every week (absences get you kicked out after a while) through to national and localised groups where you pay as you go.

The key reason why networking exists is for you to make new friends, connect people, tell people about your business and find new sources of business.

Every networking meeting is run differently, they all have a different format, the hosts are connected in different ways in the local community but the reason they exist is to do business.

Check out what local events are happening near you by going online and searching for "networking meetings in ..." which will give you your local events.

Remember a few key rules about going to a networking meeting:

a) **Take plenty of business cards.**
b) **Have a 30-second elevator pitch** so when people ask you what you do, you can tell them succinctly and clearly.

Here's an example:

"You know how some people struggle to achieve their goals and make the cash they really deserve in spite of themselves? I'm the guy that helps guide investors and business owners and gives them a clear roadmap to help them make more money."

Or how about:

"You know how some people struggle to let out their property to a good tenant who keeps the place clean and tidy, pays the rent on time and doesn't give you any hassle? I'm the woman helping investors to find a good quality tenant and offering a hassle-free management service so they can concentrate on finding more properties and not dealing with the hassle of tenants for less money than it would cost you to do it themselves."

Or how about:

"You know how some investors struggle to find motivated seller leads or decent below market value deals? I'm the guy that finds these for investors in [area], manages the buying process and at the end pops in a good quality paying tenant for you."

These are just examples but you get the idea; think about what you do, what you are offering and also more importantly how you can help other people.

People are always interested in what you can do for them so follow up your elevator pitch after they have asked you more questions about what you do with the following question:

What do you do and what are you looking for today?

This question allows them to tell you what they do and what they are looking for.

It may be you know somebody that's also looking for the same thing that your new friend is offering - so put the two of them together.

A lot of business is done at networking events through reciprocal introductions and referrals which leads to the next rule:

c) **Aim to pass on three referrals per meeting**. This allows you to be known as the person connecting people and others will be more likely to want to do business with, and pass business to, you.

d) **Have a reason for going and make sure everybody knows your reason**.

If you are looking for a JV partner, then let people know.
If you are looking for help with your first deal, then let people know.
If you are looking for a good builder, then let people know.

If you are going because you want to learn from the speaker and the topic they are talking about, ask as many questions as you can, get on their mailing list, buy their products and let people know.

Follow these rules and you will have a lot of fun at networking meetings and also do some business.

Events

There are lots of events that you can attend to give your ideas, information and networking at the same time.

Some larger events include the large property shows arranged around the UK where there will be lots of exhibitors together with the opportunity to attend talks on a variety of topics. If you are just getting started you go to these to gather information and seek advice from the different exhibitors for you to determine your path to success.

There are also local events run by the council for landlords which are always worth attending as you will be able to make contacts with the people in housing, environmental health and local housing charities.

The best way to find out about these is to ring your local Housing team up at the council.

There are also other larger events that crop up from time to time.

Typically a lot of these will be what is known as multi-speaker platform events. This means that there will be a lot of speakers on stage and at the end of each talk, they will be offering you something to buy.

Often these 'upsells' as they are known offer some extremely valuable products and services but if you are still unsure about what you want to do in the property game, then consider waiting until the end of the day and making a decision then if you want to buy something.

If you've already decided on your two or three strategies, listen closely to the speakers who are experts in the field you want to get into or are in, see if they resonate with you, evaluate if the product is for you and if it will help you move forward. If it does, go and invest in their product or service and **make sure you use it**.

I've lost count of the things I've bought that I've never used.

Applications

Nowadays there is an app for everything and if you have got a smartphone, you are spoiled for choice in terms of what you can load on to your device.

But let's look at what business apps are out there that can help you in your property investment journey.

GoToMeeting/Zoom allows you to join webinars from your phone or tablet.

Rightmove. The biggest portal has its own app to perform searches, filter and save properties on the road.

Letting Check / The Inventory Manager (TIM). If you do inventories, these apps help you perform an inventory, categorising photos you shoot into appropriate rooms and creating a PDF for everyone to sign. This cuts out a lot of work.

CloudOn. Create, use and access Microsoft Word, Excel and PowerPoint documents on the road.

Mindjet Maps. The premier software for Mind maps are curiously free via an app. Get it and use it for creating mind maps of your projects, ideas and goals.

Simplenote. A better more flexible version of the standard "Notes" to use for creating documents.

WordPress. If you have a WordPress site, use this to upload new content.

Dropbox. Free cloud data storage you can access anywhere.

Banking apps to manage your accounts, payments and debits on the road.

Moves tracks your steps and gives you data between travel points.

iTranslate never be at a loss for words again if you have to speak another language

Evernote one of my favourites, write notes, add pictures, draw a sketch and send via cloud.

FiLMiC Pro the best app for taking short videos to get the lighting and contrast just right

There are many more and these are just a taster to get you started.

Which ones are you using? Let me know and I'll update this section.

Day 20: Your Organisation

Essential to the success of your business is putting in place an organisation and robust structures to ensure that your team can operate without you.

Every business with a strong operational team and structure will succeed. The key place to begin is with your organisation.

Michael E Gerber discusses this in his book The E-Myth Revisited. He tells us:

> *"Most companies organise around personalities rather than around functions"* (Gerber, 1995, p. 167)

Most people never think of this before they get into business. They have an idea, rush to implement something, wonder why it doesn't work and then move on to something else.

That's why I heartily recommend that before you decide to rush headlong into a new business or even if you are in one right now, you take a few hours out to really focus on your business and its organisation.

What do I mean by organisation?

Your business needs to have an organisation plan for how you are going to run your business.

Don't think of what your business looks like today, but how you'll run it in the future. Five to ten years from now is an ideal starting place.

Think of the different roles needed to run your business.

Do you need someone to look after the finance side?

Do you need someone focusing on sales?

Do you need somebody that manages the operational elements of a business such as staff, out callers, handymen etc.?

Do you need an administrator to pull together all of the paperwork and keep everything running smoothly?

Spend some time and think about all of the positions you will need.

So, for instance, if you are looking to run a portfolio of 10 properties to provide for your longer term retirement, maybe this organisation would be suited to you.

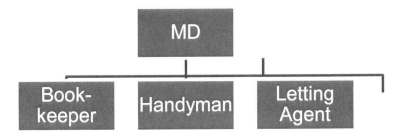

This may not be the perfect organisation for you but what it is designed to show is that to run a business a decade from now, these are the type of roles you may need in place.

Or, if you are focused on running a property business that sources properties for other clients while running a small portfolio of your own, then consider the following organisation chart.

It's not necessarily about who is going to do these roles, but what your organisation should look like to succeed.

The tricky part once you've actually done this though is to put you and your current business partners (if any) into each of the slots.

So, let's look at a husband and wife partnership who want to grow a portfolio business in their local university town focusing on students and young professionals.

The organisation and the subsequent roles may be allocated as follows:

You will see that the roles are split 4/3 in favour of the husband but this is just an example.

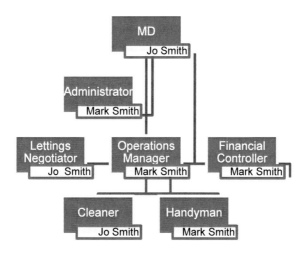

You may have more than one business partner, you may have none, but by putting down on paper your organisational chart, you can move to the next step which is creating a process map for each position.

Start on the lowest level position and look at what the person does, their responsibilities, what can be put into a process and structure that others can follow; and from this an operations manual is created for this position.

For this organisation, start with either the cleaner or the administrator.

Once you have created the basic operations manual, process flow and systems, you can look to either outsource or hire somebody to help you. They may not be a full-time person, they may not be in this country, they may be bartering services for something you can do for them but you can only put yourself in this position by creating an operations manual for that position.

I talk more about people and getting the right person in the People section of this book.

Now it's your turn to have a go to create your own organisational map.

Day #21 – Operations

Operations is what runs the company and makes everything work in the most optimised fashion.

In The E-Myth Revisited Gerber discussed at length the idea that any business can be turned from a small business into a turn-key business to be franchised, and in so doing so provides the franchisee with an entire system of doing business (Gerber, 1995).

He also said the true product of a business is the business itself, and once you understand this you can master and achieve anything you wish.

There are however some fundamentals necessary to make this change from hobbyist to serious business owner.

Guidelines

You've already done your vision statement. Now you need to translate this into a set of guidelines that staff work to <u>and</u> buy into.

By guidelines, I mean the very ethos and understanding under which you operate your business.

Do you want all staff members to answer the phone within seven rings?

Do you want a response to emails within 24 hours?

Do you want a personalised answerphone message on company mobiles as opposed to the awful generic message given to you by the mobile operators?

Do you have a dress code for staff?

These issues and many more are things to consider when starting up your business as they by their very nature will begin to create a culture within your company through which staff will either be nurtured or swamped.

If it's just you to begin with, you should still write a list because you need to hold yourself accountable. If you fail to live up to even the standards you set yourself, you will find it difficult to recruit and hold onto good staff.

So let's start the ball rolling by giving you some generic guidelines to think about:

Human Resources

 Staff dress

 Communications

 Travelling

 Mobile Phones and Laptops

 Expense Policy

 Monies

 Social Media

Sales

    Response times

    Appointments and Meetings

    Monies

Marketing

    Social Media

    Tracking

    Email marketing

    Blogs

    Websites

Finance

    Accounts

These are just some to think about but start by thinking about the type of organisation you wish to run, how you wish to be portrayed and how you can implement your guidelines into your business.

Take some pages in your journal and jot down some immediate thoughts as to which ones are the most relevant and important to you.

Pre-prepared letters

Often I find that businesses are doing the same thing over and over again and do not have a specific set of template letters in place that they can use.

Use templates that already exist, either from an outsourced supplier such as the HR and Legal outsourcers I mention in Chapter X or through downloading them at the website:

www.crackingthepropertycode.com/bookbonuses101

The time you will save in spending half a day preparing letters that you know you will be sending out time and time again will yield you dividends in the future.

File them either online so everybody can use them or if it's just you in one specific folder on your desktop. I know it sounds crazy but believe you me, not everybody does this and spends 5 minutes trying to find a file they have already created.

Follow a specific format of naming these documents such as

TEMPLATE_Tenant Welcome Letter rev1.1

LETTER_Landlord DM Letter 1 rev 1.1

SPREADSHEET_Generic Invoice rev 1.1

This way, you know that when you need to find something, you can go straight to your templates folder and then select the form that you want.

What template letters do you think you need right now to get cracking with your business?

Pre-prepared posters

Again this is similar to the letters but this is in the realm of marketing.

There are certain types of marketing that you will do over and over again and this is another way of saving time and energy in order for you to quickly produce a poster.

For instance, if you let your own properties and advertise locally, then create a generic poster that allows you to just insert the contents as and when required.

There may be things that change such as the picture, address details, rental amount and description - but your phone number and address details will not.

Take some time out to think about these posters and get them prepared today.

Holidays

Everybody needs holidays.

There is a tendency when people get started to not take any holidays. This will work for a while but there comes the moment when burnout approaches when you are working longer and longer but getting less and less done.

My recommendation is to plan in your holidays now for the next 12 months. Now for those of you who are a little spontaneous you may not like this but you can still be spontaneous about where you go.

Make a list of the weeks out that you wish to take and when and probably some long weekends too. If you aim for at least two full weeks off and two long weekends, then at least you will have these in your plan and you know that you can work towards these dates as deadlines in your diary.

Don't plan them in and you will keep putting them off and off and off.

Complete when your holidays will be in your workbook:

If you have staff, then I'd suggest getting a Staff Holidays Calendar – either keep it in a Google calendar or get one of the big boards that you can put in the office.

It's important to know when people are going to be off so that you can plan for their work to be covered.

Don't allow staff to go off on holiday without having a briefing with them and whoever will be covering their work before they go.

Call outs

Depending on what type of property business you are running, you will need to set up some kind of call out system for those emergences where everything goes wrong.

There are a few ways in which you can do this and depending on how you wish to run your organisation will depend on the result that you choose:

a) Get a pay as you go mobile phone for emergency call outs separate to your normal phone. Leave it charged up and on during your out of office hours.
b) Use a telephone answering service to take out of office calls and relay them to your normal mobile via text or email.
c) Have a staff member responsible for out of hours call outs.
d) Give tenants the details of a reliable handyman who will take out of hours emergency calls and resolve the issue (if you have one that you trust enough to do this).

It's important to set this up from the start in the way you'd like to operate so that everybody knows where they are and what the processes are.

Don't move a tenant in only for them wonder about how they get hold of you if there is an emergency.

Cloud system

Working with a team is great but most organisations do not start off with a server and CAT cables and all that gubbins.

But as small businesses we do need to make sure that documents and projects are shared.

So what's the best way to do this?

I generally find that there are a lot of free resources out there that enable you to do this and one of the very best I've found is Google Business Apps.

http://tinyurl.com/ctpc-google

This allows you to essentially manage your:

- Email
- Calendar
- Documents
- Sites
- Images
- Contacts
- Groups

And plenty of other applications you may need.

But it becomes even more powerful than that when you sync it up with your computer.

Through Google business apps, I can sync my Microsoft Outlook mail and calendar with the server which enables me to view this on my IPhone (or another smartphone that connects with this technology).

Any updates on either my IPhone or PC are then synced back to the cloud through Google Business Apps.

There is a paid-for and a free version and to be honest most small businesses will be fine with the free version. Try it and see what you think.

Dealing with complaints

In any business, we cannot deliver our best 100% of the time and there will occasionally be complaints.

Before you start getting panicky or even affronted that a client dare complain, put yourself in the shoes of your client and try to understand why they've complained and what you can do to help resolve their issue and ideally delight them so that they come back again to you and purchase more.

Start off by having a very simple Complaint Procedure in place. This can be as simple as an email address or phone number with how to complain and what information you will need in order to complain. You can then set the clients' expectations in terms of how you will resolve their issue, timeframes and likely response.

By having this in place now, you will save time creating this once a client does complain, or takes a long time trying to find out how to complain so they get a response.

What complaint systems are you going to put in place?

Consumer awareness guides

The final piece of the jigsaw is optional, but one in which you will find a lot of value if you decide to use it.

Most clients want to know that they are dealing with a reputable, honest, ethical and caring organisation.

They want to know that the business they are doing business with has experience and knows what they are doing.

One of the simplest ways in which you can ensure that consumers know this is by creating a Consumer Awareness Guide.

This doesn't have to be a work of fiction but ideally should be a short guide on your industry niche to illustrate what a consumer should look out for when purchasing from someone in the industry.

Typical areas to focus on would be the industry, why to buy, what to ask, fees involved, any regulations and information about your company.

Here's a brief example:

Example – Letting To Professionals

- Introduction to Letting a Property
- Why Rent A Property
- What To Ask When Viewing Properties

- Typical Fees Involved in Renting A Property
- Regulations On Letting Properties
- About XYZ Company

What consumer awareness guide do you think you can create?

What would be included in it?

I hope that this section has given you a good idea of what to think about and do when setting up your Operations team and that you've followed the steps I've illustrated to get kicked off as quickly as possible when you launch your business.

Stage #3 of the 5 Stage Blueprint

Cultivate

STAGE #3 CULTIVATE
Day 22: Sales

Think of this as the power plant of your business as this is where your business becomes exciting and real whereas where this is ignored, issues rise and business stagnates.

This is not just about clients however; it can be used in any area of your life; relationships, sports, health, children and of course our businesses.

I have lost track over the years of the enquiries I have made for products and services only for me not to be contacted back.

In the last year, I've enquired and am still waiting to hear back from:

- A publishing consultancy regarding help with new book projects
- An eco-firm with new technology to help with reducing costs in HMO's
- Virtual Assistants who didn't follow up on my detailed response back to them
- An SEO and tech firm on a proposal for managing my websites and tech support
- A highly regarded "marketer" on a business opportunity
- An energy company regarding consolidation of suppliers

And this is probably just the tip of the iceberg when I think of other things that I was interested in.

Remember this – it is four times as difficult to get a new client than it is to keep an existing one – but every potential new "prospect" may be your new best client.

It takes a great deal of effort to find a new client but it takes as much effort to nurture and cultivate your client so that they become lifelong fans.

Most businesses ignore this and at their peril.

But this can be very easily remedied by ensuring that you have a client cultivation plan in place.

This can be taken at a very basic level by looking at the different ways in which we treat a client, how we acquire a client and how we then communicate with a client going forward.

Part of the process we go through in the 100K Club is creating our clients lifecycle and journey and for the next part; let's quickly look at this in terms of what you should be considering having in place to manage your client lifecycle process:

1. Do you have a good understanding of the entry points that your client will first be made aware of your business?

2. Once your client has made initial contact with you, what steps are you taking to introduce your business, products and how you can help them in your journey

3. How do you keep in contact?

4. How do you ensure that your company is kept in their mind when they come to a point of wanting to purchase a product which you offer (and not go to your competitors)

5. How do you come from a place of wanting to give first knowing that profits will flow to you

These are just a few of the questions to ask out of a 17 point checklist but gives you an idea of how detailed you need to get about your client.

Clients are a gift, a treasure that should be lovingly looked after and to all intents and purpose have to be an investment for both the now and the future.

Without them, our businesses cannot flourish and without treating them correctly, our businesses will not grow.

Often this is ignored at the bequest of profits, busyness or more urgent things to do but it's important that we remember.

A client is not just for now, a client is for life.

If we take this attitude and treat them with the care and attention that they deserve, then they will go onto become lifelong clients and ultimately raving fans of ours that will spearhead our growth through word of mouth and referrals.

Quick Win.

Spend five minutes brainstorming your entry points to your business, the different media channels you use, the lifecycle that a client goes through and maybe from this create your ideal client.

Without sales, you'll wither and die. Trust me, we really don't want that. Take heart, be focused and the sales will come.

We often find ourselves talking about sales as a dirty word but it really isn't. Sales at its heart is about finding solutions to issues raised by consumers or businesses and finding the solution to those issues. It's not about ramming a product that's not wanted down somebody's throat for them to unwillingly part with money.

Sales is an important job and it reminds of a quote from a book a long time ago that is essential for us to remember in our business.

> *Nothing happens anywhere in the world until a sale takes place. And salespeople bring in the money that everyone else can eventually live off. (Denny, 1997)*

In this section, I cover strategies which you can use in order to make sure that you are dealing with the right clients and that you are making the most out of your offering.

Before we do that, here are some questions that you need to consider in order to launch your business and start making sales as swiftly as possible.

What is your product?

What does the product look, feel, taste and smell like?

How does it satisfy your clients' needs and wants?

Who is your ideal client?

Demographically, who are they?

How old are they? Where do they live? How much do they earn? Where do they hang out? What media are they influenced by? What are their interests?

If you had a magic wand and could give them anything that they want - what would it be?

With regard to your topic, what do they want? What do they need?

What are they afraid of? What frustrates them?

What do they lose sleep over at night?

What will be their biggest objections to doing business with you?

Understanding the answers will enable us to approach the next section dealing with how we qualify, win and keep clients and focus on the top 20% who are giving us 80% of the business.

I encourage you to take the time out to think about the above questions and start formulating your answers as it is easier to do now than it is when you have launched and suddenly have clients to deal with.

Qualifying

Once you have identified your ideal client, ensure you are going to qualify them correctly to do business with you.

This criteria can take many forms and I have listed some examples below for you to consider depending on different business types (remember you should by this point have decided on one to three strategies to pursue so bear this in mind when thinking about your own qualification criteria).

Professional Houseshare Lets

1. Over 21
2. Single
3. Job paying over £15,000 per year
4. Guarantor
5. Deposit
6. Long term tenant
7. No contractors

First Time Investors

1. Deposit of 25%
2. Good credit score

3. Some education (minimum of one quality book and one seminar)
4. Location Generic
5. Interested in cashflow or pension
6. Use our packaging team

Letting Agent

1. 1 to 3-bed flats and terraces
2. Focus on LHA tenants
3. Focus on Council / Universal Credit expertise
4. No deposits
5. Families or single mothers
6. Over 18s
7. Long-term tenants

Now complete Your Criteria in your journal.

Now that you have some ideas on qualification, the next route is in acquiring new clients.

New clients
The hardest part of any business is finding your new client.

Most of the marketing costs are used to attract people to your shop, store, office and website where some will go to do business with you.

It's your job to ensure that the largest number of possible potential clients that fit your qualification criteria do go onto do business with you.

So how do you do this?

The hardest part is having something that people want in order to give up their details.

For many businesses, the first place they will start nowadays is online.

We'll talk more about your website in the next chapter but for now, think of something that you can give away for free as a lead magnet in order to attract new clients to you.

If you're in lettings, it may be a guide to letting a house the easy way.

If you're in sourcing, it may be a guide to how to source a house in less than 30 days.

If you're in buy-to-let, it may be a guide to finding the right property for you.

If you're in lease options, it may be a guide to getting rid of your debt and mortgage problems within 30 days.

There are lots and lots of different things that you can do but it is has been proven through many studies that offering a free report, video, audio or briefing will allow prospective clients to connect with you and to start interacting with you.

So, let's take some time to think about what your free report may look like by following these open questions designed to get you to think.

What is the major problem that your clients face in your market?

What very simple guide could you put together that solves these problems?

What 3, 5 or 7 ways could you illustrate that give your client information that if they wished to, would allow them to go out and do it for themselves (don't worry, 1 out of 4 may do but most want you to do it for them)?

Now think of some headlines for your free giveaway enticing people to run and push and jostle others out of the way to get it.

Here are some thoughts to get you going:

The 5 Secrets To...

7 Killer Ways To...

Discover the 3 Ways To...

Now write a few of your own:

Now that you have a headline or two to consider, the next exercise is to write some copy for the report, ideally following this template.

Introduction

The 3, 5 or 7 ideas you wish to share

Ending and Your Offer and how you can help people further

This will by far generate more leads and clients for you than any other form of sales that you can get started with straight away.

It's something that you can give away on your website, as a printed brochure/booklet, on a CD, business card links – the possibilities are endless.

Use your journal to note down some comments on how you can do this.

Current clients

For those that are already in business, you may have existing clients.

These clients need looking after but firstly, we need to do an exercise to look at the revenue verses time spent on the clients to understand who is bringing in the lion's share of the revenue for you.

Take half an hour to get all of your clients listed onto a spreadsheet with the amounts they are currently spending with you.

Then look at the time spent on each client – this doesn't need to be exact but is to give you an idea of the approximate time. Use it in hours and half hours if you can.

Then put in an extra column and divide the revenue by the number of hours.

So for instance, if you have a client paying you £5,000 per year and you spend 1 hour a month on them, that's 12 hours per year. Divide the £5,000 by 12, and you're making £416.66 an hour.

If you have another client who spends £1,000 per year and you spend 3 hours per month on them (36 hours a year), divide the £1,000 by 12 and you get £83.33 per hour.

The reason for doing this is to identify the clients making you the most money so you can find more of them.

At the same time, it is essential to know who your less profitable clients are so that you can start to create strategies to minimise the amount of time and effort that you are spending on them.

It will never be possible to have just highly profitable, low time-intensive clients, but it is possible to change the percentages so you have more profitable clients paying you more money.

Once you've identified who your top 20% clients are; start to think about how you can service them better and make them feel like the VIPs they are.

Use a spreadsheet to do this and then answer the following questions:

What is your average spending per client?

How much profit does this generate per year/month/week?

What percentage of your top clients give you 80% of your revenue?

Which clients take up the most time – and why?

What profile do you top clients take – and why?

Sales Process

I will discuss this more in the Systems section but one area I have found invaluable over the last 20 years I've been in business is having a process in place to automate some aspects of what you are doing on a daily basis.

A must is some form of Client Relationship Management software. There are many on the market such as Salesforce, Goldmine and Act although there is another I recommend above all of these that I will be talking about in the Systems section.

What a CRM solution allows you to do is to capture the details of your clients in one central database. But it does much more than that.

It allows you to:

- Reduce costs - because the right things are being done (more effective and efficient operations)
- Increase client satisfaction - because they are getting exactly what they want (and you exceed expectations)

- Grow your client base
- Maximise opportunities (increase services and referrals)
- Increase access to market and competitor information
- Highlight poor operational processes
- Improve long term profitability and sustainability

At its heart, a CRM system will contain information on your client but rather than just their contact details, it could include information such as what they have bought, what products interest them, but haven't yet been bought, what emails they have opened, what they've clicked, when their last contact was with you and with which member of staff, notes on the last conversation you had with them, and more.. This allows you to become much more focused on the right set of clients who are going to become more profitable for you on a long-term basis.

Even if you don't have a system as complex as this, having some basic sales processes in place is going to help ensure that you are being more efficient and effective than your competitors so think about putting processes in place for:

- Calling, emailing and mailing landlords
- Calling, emailing and mailing tenants
- Property leads

This means you can operate the same system on a continuous basis and not have to rely upon doing something as the spur of the moment comes to you.

It means that you can also review the results.

Take some time out now to note down some things that you do on a daily basis that you could create a small sales process around. These are anything that you are doing in day-in and day-out to generate sales that can be put into a simple process or automated.

1.

2.

3.

4.

5.

Day 23: Marketing

Marketing is probably my favourite activity of all. It can really make the difference between your success and failure.

To some, marketing is a black art. To others it's the colouring-in department. Elsewhere it's seen as a way to get people to know more about the business.

Marketing is a communications activity allowing prospective clients to get to know you better and decide whether to buy. Your job is to persuade them to buy from you and not your competition.

Hugh Davidson puts this elegantly when he states the key principles of marketing should be based around POISE:

- **Profitable** - the proper balance between the firms need for profit and the clients need for value
- **Offensive** - you must lead the market, take risks and make competitors followers
- **Integrated** - your marketing approach must permeate the whole company
- **Strategic** - probing analysis leading to a winning strategy
- **Effectively Executed** - strong and disciplined execution on a daily basis.

(Davidson, 1997)

There are many ways to do this and included in the next chapter are a raft of different strategies that you can undertake in order to get your business out there and noticed.

I'd encourage you to take these 10 strategies and work through them one at a time.

I'd also recommend that you take out your journal for this section and make some notes and answer some of the questions I'm going to be asking.

1. Website

Do you have a website?

If not, then you need one.

Today's websites are yesterday's shops. It's your shop front to let people know exactly what you do, why you do it and more importantly what's in it for them.

There are websites and there are websites.

Ideally you need to be aiming between being attractive and functional. Too much design and you end up with a funky website that cannot be used. Too much functionality and the user gets confused.

In order of importance of what to aim for and think about for your website, here are some pointers to consider:

a) Is your web address a clear indication of what you do? hmofurniturepackages.co.uk does what it says on the tin - it's HMO furniture that landlord can buy in packages. Yourhmoexpert.com is a website all about HMO topics.

b) Can what you do be summed up in a nice easy to remember and search friendly relevant phrase? If you buy houses quickly in Bristol, could your website be bristolfasthomebuyers.com? If you offer cleaning services in Aberdeen for landlords could your website be aberdeenlandlordcleaningservices.co.uk?

c) what message are you trying to get across? Is it clear, is it concise, can you summarise it within five bullet points?

d) Can a 12 year-old understand your website? Do you use easy to understand language that most people will understand?

e) Do you have an opt-in box so that you can capture people's details and communicate with them? It's important to have this so that you can build a list as a list can become a community who become your fans and thus will purchase from you in the future.

f) Do you have a free report, eBook, video, audio, voucher, discount or other offer that appeals to users enough to want to give you their name and email address?

g) Is your content relevant to your website? If you have a website called bristolfasthomebuyers.com, is your website all about buying in Bristol? Don't start talking about lease options or how you offer inventories or EPCs to landlords, as this is a different business entirely and needs a different website.

h) Do you have social media linked into your website (see the separate social media section later on)? In today's age, you have to have these integrated into your site.

i) Do you have a clear About Us page that tells people about who you and what you do and why you are doing it? People want to interact with people and the worst thing you can do is create a corporate site that has no look and feel and doesn't allow anybody to know who is behind the company and why they do what they do.

j) Do you have a clear Contact Us page and can people get hold of you via email, phone and mail? The more detail you have here, the more likely it is that people will want to do business with you.

k) Do you have a good mixture of photographs and text that make it easy for people to consume?

There are plenty of ways in which you can create a website.

By far the most popular nowadays is ones using content management systems such as WordPress which allow you to upload their software on to your server and create your own content the way you wish it to look.

It requires a bit of jiggery-pokery to get a website looking good but 90% of it you can do yourself. The other 10% you can easily get somebody off one of the technical sites I recommend.

Try it out – you'll be surprised at what you can do

13 Things You Should Consider With Your Website	Go On – Give Me A Tick When You've Done Me!
Create One Worth Bookmarking	
Who are you? Tell a story.	
Tell clients exactly what to expect.	
Ask your clients for testimonials	
Create a funny 404 page	
Include a smiley picture	
Write copy around the message	
Include a greeting "happy xx day"	
Use a clear landing page that tells clients what you do	
Make it easy for visitors to subscribe via an opt-in form.	
Choose a domain name you are proud of and imagine shouting from a mountain.	
Add an Easter egg (something that takes a bit of finding but makes people	

smile when they do).	
Create an exceptional user experience.	

2.Social media

If you are not on social media you are losing traffic, leads and sales.

Over 80% of those under 24 are using social media. Even as people get older, people are still using these channels with 30% of over 60s online.

Age Range	% Using Social Media
18-29	83%
30-49	70%
50-64	51%
65+	33%

Source: (Pew Research Center, Feb 2005, Aug 2006, May 2008, April 2009, May 2010, May 2011)

The main channels you can use are many and varied but here are some of the favourites right now:

Facebook

LinkedIn

Google+

Twitter

Whichever channels you decide to use, here are some important points that you NEED To be aware of and using.

Getting Your Brand On Social Media

We talked about this in a previous chapter but it's important that whatever branding you went with, this needs to be representative on social media.

There is little point in having branding that does not match up.

Use the platforms your clients and prospects are using

Be clear about what platforms your clients may be on.

For instance, LinkedIn is generally full of businesspeople looking to connect whilst Facebook has people who want to be entertained.

Twitter has people that want short snappy updates. Google+ has until very recently had a lot of techies hanging out but this is now changing with the advent of new features and ways of hanging out attracting a younger audience.

Do some research first before jumping in.

Don't talk about your "brand strategy", but instead focus on interacting

It's important you don't just join a forum or discussion and start talking about your brand.

What is more important is that you give considered opinion as to what you are doing, how you see changes in your market and how you can help people who may be struggling.

Use the same profile picture across different sites

Consistency is key here. Whatever social channels you find yourself on, you must ensure that you use the same picture for your profile picture (or gravatar).

Often people on social media will use a couple of networks to interact and it makes it much easier for them if you are present on different sites with the same image. This consistency also lends an air of professionalism.

We are aiming to use social media here as a business growth tool so be careful of the type of picture you use but make sure you use one that does feature you and is not a caricature of someone else, picture of an animal or even worse - somebody else.

Thank your readers, friends, followers, and clients for sharing your content

One of the ways in which social media becomes its own animal is in the way that your readers will share your content.

Sharing is social proof to other people who may not necessarily know you but will have your content recommended by their friends.

Get them to comment on your content and in turn, comment on their content.

When you start building up a sizeable following this can become more difficult to manage but by following the steps we mention below, you can manage most of this in 15 minutes a day.

Share great content from numerous authors

A great way into getting conversations going and having people start to follow you is to share interesting content from different authors.

Be aware of sharing content that is perhaps very similar to yours unless it compliments it but if you can share other respected authority figures content, this will serve you well in positioning you as the go-to expert for your niche.

Do more listening than tweeting, updating, and posting

This is really key. There is nothing worse than jumping in and just putting out nonsense on the social media channels.

Think about what you want to say before you say

But more importantly, listen to what others are saying. And then comment on other conversations that are going on by adding value to them.

Join a group on LinkedIn

There are dozens of groups on LinkedIn that you can join and start contributing to. It is worth joining a few at a time to dive into the conversations, get a feel for the group, the level of activity and then decide whether you wish to then get involved and start contributing.

By contributing regularly, you build up content that others can refer to and this also allows you to be in touch with the movers and shakers in your industry.

Choose a specific purpose for using Twitter

Will you be using Twitter to share content, news stories, videos, special offers and discount coupons? Decide on your main focus for using Twitter and stick to it. If you want people to join a deal of the day list, don't confuse them by offering them content on your product as well. The two do not mix.

I've include an inspirational poster on the following page which you can also download at the bonus section for book owners at:

www.crackingthepropertycode.com/book1bonuses

Source: (Dunn, 2013)

Social Media Plan

Bearing in mind that it is easy to get confused, I've laid out the bare fundamentals right now of what you need to be doing.

These are affectionately known as the three Cs of social media:

Community – you need to grow your following and your reach

Content – you need to put stuff out there that will be seen but also responded too

Conversations – you need to have 2-way conversations with others.

By focusing overall on these three areas, your social media presence will rapidly grow.

Here's how to do it in just 15 minutes a day:

Block	Time Spent	Focus
1st	5 minutes	Community
2nd	5 minutes	Conversations
3rd	5 minutes	Content

Source: (Hatch, 2012)

The detail on what to do is as follows.

Community needs to be focused upon building your list.

You can do this in a few ways:

- Leverage your existing list by building a social media Like and Share buttons to get people interacting with you online
- Create a Facebook or LinkedIn advert to drive traffic to your page
- Follow, comment and respond to industry leaders on Twitter

Conversations need to be focused on having good conversations.

This requires

a) speaker
b) message
c) listener

Engage in conversations already happening through a social media management dashboard such as Hootsuite, to look at a broader reach of what's happening across the various channels.

Start your own conversations.

Be transparent and responsive.

Content needs to be engaging, shareable and worthy of comments.

Where do you get this from?

You can use other people's content which you reword to your own purposes; or write a blog post (see the next section).

The key here is to start doing it and to have a goal in mind in terms of how you are going to grow your community, conversations and content.

Here's an example from the chief trainer at Infusionsoft on how to do it.

	Community	Conversations	Content
2 Week Goal	20% increase in the number of followers on Facebook and Twitter	Ask 2 questions on Twitter Ask 2 questions on Facebook	20 tweets 1 blog post 15 retweets
1 Month Goal	500 Twitter followers and 100 likes on Facebook	Run a poll with 150 responses	3 blog posts, 100 tweets and 15 retweets of your content

(Hatch, 2012)

1. Blogging and Authority Sites

At its heart, a blog is an online journal.

It's a way of sharing your thoughts, opinions and ideas with the wider world.

It enables anybody to have an online presence without having to know computer code and it's almost as simple as using email. Best of all, blog software nowadays is generally free with the leading platform WordPress.org

There are literally millions of blogs online and it can become confusing for the prospective reader to know where to go to find out the latest information on a specific topic.

The best way to start distinguishing yourself from other blogs is by focusing upon a niche and becoming an authority in that niche by giving away free information.

What this leads to is free exposure and gets you website from a variety of sources.

You can check out an example of a niche site at yourhmoexpert.com which still receives around 2,000 visitors a month despite it not being updated often with new content.

The reason why you need to choose a niche is so that you can become the authority on that particular market and start capturing traffic who are looking for your niche.

It is important that for a blog to gather new traffic that you post regular content onto your blog.

There are many ways you can generate content.

- Private Label Rights articles
- Free Articles from Article Directories

- Public Domain Content
- Write it yourself

Whatever source of content you choose, the content needs to be relevant, interesting and keep your readers coming back to your blog.

While you may pick up on a news story and use this as a basis for your blog; you don't have to post it verbatim but use it as a starting point for your views on the particular story.

In order to start gathering traffic, you can promote your blog via:

- Social Media
- Email List
- Website
- Press Releases
- Exchanging Links
- Articles
- Directories

You also need to set up a capture box to get people's names and email addresses. Without this, you cannot continue building the relationship with your readers and you lose out on valuable potential prospects.

For reliable email providers I recommend either GetResponse or Aweber, both which have Lite versions to try.

You can use a subscriber capture form on your website which is often included with blogging software. I wouldn't recommend it as it's far too easy to have emails sent out from this software to be put in the spam folder.

Once you have captured somebody's details, you need to enter them into what is known as an auto-responder series. What this does is send out an automated email over a pre-defined period of time – normally 30 days.

This helps automate your business (which we'll talk more about in Systems) and generate more income for you.

Setting up a blog does take some time but you can often find people who can help you with some of the trickier elements on the outsourcing websites which we'll cover in another chapter.

For more information, I can't recommend any source more highly than Jack Humphrey's Authority Black Book – check him out for top tips on how to build your site to become an authority in your niche.

(Humphreys, 2011)

2. Advertising

Advertising at its simplest form is a way of getting your message out there so that people know who you are, what you do and how they can get in contact with you.

These three elements are critical and I will repeat them again so that you ensure that any advert you do has these three elements.

a) Who are you – what's your company name?
b) What do you do – what exactly is it that you do? How do you do it? Why should they do business with you?
c) How do they get in contact with you – you need to ensure that you have contact details so that people can call, email or go onto your website.

There are many forms of advertising that we can use to promote our business.

Some reasonable low-cost ways of getting your message out there include the following.

Leaflets

A leaflet has to grab people's attention. It has to stand out.

It's often said that you have seven seconds to capture somebody's attention and in today's distracting and bombarding world; it's probably even less.

What are the key things that we need to do on a leaflet?

We need to grab their attention.

Think of this as us basically getting somebody's attention very quickly - almost like if you were walking down the street and you suddenly spot something that draws your attention such as a poster, a car, a busker, loud music, an attractive member of the opposite sex. Whatever it may be it draws your attention quickly.

Headlines

Think of when you last read a paper or magazine or watched the TV. Which adverts or headlines drew your attention?

They are the ones which use words which are:

- Shocking
- Cut through the crap
- Make a bold statement
- Appeal to emotion
- Offer something
- Unexpected

Go and buy a newspaper right now, ideally a tabloid, and look through the pages and circle the ads that stand out to you.

These are the types of headlines that you want on your leaflets.

So, we could have:

WARNING: Your Home Is 2 Payments Away From Repossession

90% Of Landlords Do Not Make Any Money – Are You One Of Them?

29 Year Old Former Homeless Lorry Driver Discovers How to Make £1,000 Per Month From One Property

Only 5 People Will Qualify For This New Mastermind Programme

The Qualifying Questions

What we then need to focus on are the key bullet points that get our message across. Ideally no more than 5-7 as too many and the reader will get confused.

So taking the first headline, we could do the following:

WARNING: Your Home Is 2 Payments Away From Repossession

- Struggling with your debts?
- Living from day to day with payday loans?
- Finding it difficult to keep up with your mortgage payments?
- Having issues with creditors?
- Had your hours cut at work?

Put yourself in the mind of your prospect and think about what issues they would be facing and what questions or worries they would have.

Brainstorm a list of them then choose the top five to seven and try and make them a short and snappy as possible so that they get your point across quickly.

The Offer

Once somebody has a) identified with the headline and b) answered yes to two or more of these questions, you have a chance to offer them whatever your service is.

So using the above example we could use something similar to this.

Contact Annie your local property and debt solutions advisor to discuss your issue....

- Confidential and friendly service
- No Catches – Completely Free of Charge
- Home visits available
- Available 24/7 365 days a year

Call To Action

Now we need a strong call to action to get them to contact us.

This needs to be strong enough for the people who are serious to take action right away and for those who will keep the leaflet a while to come back to it to call you..

So we could use the following:

Avoid repossession and call Annie today on XXX XXX XXX

Secure your finances and call Annie today on XXX XXX XXX

Don't put off your debt issues, call today on XXX XXX XXX

Contact Information

I'd advise having at the very minimum the following information:

A name. This doesn't have to be yours and it's been proven through testing that a female name does work better but if you do not have a female to answer the phone, put your name on.

A number. Nowadays you can choose from lots of numbers. 0800 is still not free from mobile phones, so mobile users do not like calling them. A mobile number is good. A local number for your area is also great and will work to your advantage if you want people to know that you are local.

A website. It's important to have one as some people although they are interested will want to look at your website first and may even enquire online. Make sure you've gone through the website checklist.

Email Marketing

This is one of the most popular forms of marketing and is extremely cheap.

However a lot of people do this wrong and what I want to show you in the next chapter is how to do it correctly.

What's the three ways in which we can win?

1. Get more email addresses
2. Get more emails opened
3. Get more clickthroughs

There are dozens of internet marketers that I've followed over the years but some of the very best that I've had the privilege to be mentored by include Mike Filsaime, Frank Garon, Ryan Deiss and Nikhil Parekh. They have helped me test and use many marketing tactics over the years. Check them out if you want the very latest strategies on marketing online.

What is spam?

Let's start by noting the following statement about spam.

Spam is unsolicited mail that you have sent either via post or email. In the email marketing world, spam is a big no.

If you collect 10 business cards at an event and have a conversation with these people about property and you tell them that you'll contact them to follow up, this would be fine.

If however, you enter them into your email marketing programme and start sending what is essentially unsolicited mail, then these same 10 contacts could become slightly annoyed with you and start marking your emails as spam. It could well be that only two of them actually wanted to keep in contact.

Opt-In forms

What we need to do is build a list of people that do wish to receive emails from us and are interested in what we have to say.

We do this via an opt-in form.

There are good and bad ways of doing opt-in forms.

The bad way is to hide your opt-in form on a sub-page or secondary page of your website where online visitors have to go or to have a form which says *Subscribe here to receive my newsletter*. It's not very inspiring, is it?

Every time you force your visitors to click another page to get to valuable information, you lose around 40% of them.

So if we have 100 visitors and the only way to get to your opt-in page is to go to your website, then click on a Newsletter tab (already down to 60 visitors), then click on another page which says *sign up here* (now down to 46 visitors), you will be left with just 46 people that *may* sign up to your list.

Typically, conversion rates can be anything from 10% to 80% if you have a well-crafted opt-in page with optimised qualified traffic.

From those 46 people you'd end up with anything from 5 to 37 people. But if your opt-in form was on your home page, correctly positioned with killer headlines and content, you'd be looking to capture 10% to 80% of the 100 visitors that arrived meaning potential opt-ins of 10 to 80 people.

You can see the value of how this works in terms of getting 100 visitors per day. Over the course of a month having your opt-in page on your front page would mean potentially 300 to 2,400 people signing up versus 50 to 1,110.

Now you may think that this doesn't matter too much in terms of the numbers but the other rough rule that's always been true with a list is:

The value is in the list

It's often been said that for every name on your list, you have the potential to make $1 per month provided you keep the list warm and keep sending good content as well as promoting products and services.

This means that the difference between 2,400 people and 1,110 people per month is a huge $15,480 over a year - or in UK terms, around £10,000!

Here's some tips to ensure that you get the optimum number of people opting into your list:

- Ensure your opt-in is **above-the-fold**. This is internet jargon for saying that you should not need to scroll down in order to see your opt-in form
- Have an **attention grabbing** headline

- Use **ultra-specific, benefit-rich** bullet points
- Have a definite **call-to-action**

Email Marketing Software Programmes

Often a lot of people when they are getting started use either their Gmail or business email through Outlook or similar mailing programme to mail out to clients.

Some people will use the so-called newsletter programmes within WordPress or whatever website building software they use.

DO NOT DO EITHER OF THESE THINGS!

What you need to do is use a specific email marketing programme to send out your emails.

There are many different providers but the best providers are Aweber and GetResponse. 1ShoppingCart is also good and includes a shopping cart/ecommerce facility but is more expensive. If you are serious about making email marketing and selling products online as part of your business, then I cannot recommend Infusionsoft enough which is what I currently use. More on this in the Systems chapter.

Why should you use an email marketing programme?

1) More of your emails will get through. Often emails can be stopped that are sent from your domain or your personal email address as just

ONE person has told their email provider that you have spammed them.

2) You can send emails in bulk. No putting together an email and searching for your contacts. They are all in the database and you can select sub-sets of them.

3) You can create professional templates with integrated video, pictures, audio, social media and more.

4) You can track all of your links and your database. How many opened the email, how many clicked on the links, how many unsubscribed or subscribed etc.

5) You can set up campaigns or auto-responders (i.e. a series of 7 emails that when somebody has signed up to your list, they get one per day every day for seven days).

The cost of these varies but you should be able to get a basic Lite version of these programmes for less than $20 per month – a necessary investment for you to start building your business.

Getting Your List To Open Your Emails

This is the one thing that most people forget about. Just because you have a list of 10,000 people doesn't meant to say that most people will open your email. I often have some people open up an email I sent weeks after sending it.

Open rates also vary enormously and I remember when I first got started using Infusionsoft that our success coach at the time was staggered to find out that I was averaging open rates of 30%+.

Open rates for a lot of people are below 10% and the reason is that people are busy and email is easy to ignore. And you are not getting their attention.

We could take an entire chapter or training programme just to talk about how to get people to open your emails but that's probably the genesis of another book on how to get people to want to open your emails or letters.

Here's some tips:

> **Use headlines that grab**. Use things such as odd numbers, question marks, percentages, new video, free report, RE or personally aimed pronouns or name
>
> **Time your mailings**. The best times to mail out are between Tuesday to Thursday around 4.30am so that it hits the inbox as they come into work or are still at home and is still around for the lunchtime and evening crowd who check their emails then.
>
> **Recycle your mailings**. You can track open rates so why not resend to those who haven't opened it (you need email marketing software to help you do this).

Getting Clickthroughs From Your Mailings

Now you've got people to actually open your emails; you've now got to get them to click on your links in order to get them engaged and buying from you.

From the various mailings and tests I've done over the years plus heavy investment in my own education with the experts I mentioned earlier; here are a few ways in which you can improve your clickthroughs.

Get to the point. If you're not sending out a newsletter, then why not make it short and to the point. If you can't get the nucleus of your message over in less than 400 words; you sure as hell can bet that your readers won't get it either.

Make sure your links are spread throughout your email. Put them in the introduction, the body and the close.

Use video. Video within email works wonders and I can testify that the clickthroughs on video have always been immense. Maybe use a headline within the video image to draw more readers in to click on it.

De-personalise. Sometimes being blunt and to the point and having no personalisation works. You can't do it all the time but if you are offering a new free report on something that you believe speaks for itself, just go straight into why they need it and what they need to do.

These tips in themselves won't make your mailings work straight away but they will go a long way to ensuring that you avoid common mistakes that beginners often make - and start with the end goal in sight, which is:

1. Get more email addresses
2. Get more emails opened
3. Get more clickthroughs

Promotional mailings

This is good old fashioned direct mail at its best.

It still works because often people do not expect it, are not looking for it and when they do get it, they will often read it because so few businesses send out direct mail these days. The ones that do are often thrown in the bin because they are so predictable.

There are different ways in which you can send out mailings.

From simple letters to postcards to bulky mail (with a CD or book inside) through to fold out/cut-out cards and magazines, the world is your oyster when it comes to direct mail.

The critical element with direct mail is getting the responses back.

So everything we've already talked about in terms of advertising and even email marketing needs to come into play with direct mail but in a way that people can quickly respond.

It's best to have different strategies for

a) Prospective Clients
b) Existing Clients
c) Reactivating Old Clients

These in themselves could have different ways in which you communicate.

For instance you could rank your existing clients into spend or value. We'll cover database segmentation later but you could find that you have a mailing series that mails out to existing clients according to their spend.

Day 24: Marketing Part 2

3. Client Liaison

Often we forget that if we have a business we have clients and clients are often our best source of information about how well we are doing and how we could do better.

So let's utilise this to generate more income and also create more rapport and good feeling.

Client surveys

Who knows how they feel about your business as much as clients?

Nobody.

A really insightful strategy to consider is the client survey.

Start by listing a set of questions that you would like to know the answers to (if you don't already) and think about what questions you could put in to help improve what you're offering in terms of your service or product.

Ask:

> Please rate the current service you receive from us in regards to ...

> Please rate how satisfied you are with our response to your queries

Please rate how often you use [product/service]

Please rate our business on a scale of 1 to 10 for:
Friendliness
Efficiency
Proactivity
Response

Please rate how likely you would be to recommend [product/service] to your friends or colleagues.

You may not like the answers to some of these questions but they will tell you how your clients feel and how you can improve your service or product.

Also consider what's in it for them. I often get surveys sent through to me and often I start filling them in but if it takes more than a couple of minutes I get bored and wonder what's in it for me. If you can enter them into a free prize draw or give them a discount or free product, you will get more responses.

Finally I'd recommend using an online survey tool such as surveymonkey.com to do your first survey. It will be free for the first 50 responders which is enough to give you a good sample data set.

Seminars or Client Appreciation Days

This is a great opportunity to both educate your clients on what is going on plus potentially generate sales on additional products and services.

You can hold this in your offices or hire a cheap meeting room. Then put on some food and drink and produce a nice, short presentation for your guests.

I wouldn't approach it as a training seminar but more of an update on the company, any changes, any new products or services and maybe some awards.

You can mention any product or service you have on offer at the end and have appropriate literature in place to back up your presentation.

People like meeting other people and they like meeting other people who are in the same business and have something in common. Try it out - you'll be surprised about how grateful your clients are and also how receptive they are to the event you're putting on for them.

4. USP

Having a unique selling proposition is a must in order to distinguish yourself from your competitors.

It's the difference between whether a client will do business with you or not. It's not a catchy slogan but a way of communicating to your clients what it is that you do – that nobody else does.

When I first got started with HMOs back in 2004, my USP at the time was

Executive Houseshares for Professionals

It's not the sexiest nor the most memorable, but it helped put us on the map and allowed us to focus on providing an awesome service to our clients.

Sometimes it doesn't have anything to do with your product or service but it heightens awareness, connects with consumers and makes them remember you.

Who remembers the classic Domino's Pizza USP when they launched back in the 80s?

You get fresh, hot pizza delivered to your door in 30 minutes or less -- or it's free.

It's a classic for a variety of reasons. Let's look at them:

- **Fresh** - client benefit. "I don't want old, stale pizza but I do want it cooked fresh".
- **Hot** - client benefit. It can be eaten and enjoyed immediately. This is one that often pizza takeaways fall down on as often the product arrives lukewarm and has to be warmed up in the oven.
- **Pizza** - what you are getting. It's not a vague 'meal' or 'hunger satisfied', but tells you exactly what you are getting.
- **Delivered to your door** - client benefit. This time around the convenience of the service which appeals to anyone who doesn't want to make any effort and you know what you are getting again.
- **In 30 minutes or less** - a specific promise. Domino's doesn't say 'delivered as soon as we

can', but within 30 minutes. Within 31 minutes you can be eating pizza. It's great to know your pizza is on the way as opposed to a lot of places who say 'it will be probably half an hour to 45 minutes'.

- **Or it's free** - the guarantee. A critical element but slotted in nicely to distinguish from everybody else.

Because of the amount of messages packed into such a short sentence it propelled Domino's to the number 1 slot in the US and later the UK (Simister, 2009).

This guarantee has now been dropped due to lawsuits in the US but even now it's still a strong one

If for any reasons you are dissatisfied with your Domino's Pizza dining experience, we will remake your pizza or refund your money

I can tell you from experience that they do this as I once had a pizza turn up late which was stone cold. I had a fresh hot one within 20 minutes.

So back on to creating your own USP.

It could be how you deliver a service. It could be the selection of products you have available, it could be a guarantee, or it could be based on price.

Typically there are different ways in which you can create your own USP. For this, I'm going to use the basis of Jonathan Jay's 10-step process to defining your own

USP with my own pointers to get you thinking about the right questions to ask yourself.

1. **Low Price**. Are you competing on price? Can you afford to?
2. **High Quality**. What quality do you offer that is outstanding compared to others?
3. **Superior Service**. Do you deliver your service in a way that is amazing? How do you do it?
4. **Size/Selection**. Is your selection better, or is your product bigger, than the competition?
5. **Convenience**. How easy is it to access your product?
6. **Knowledgeable Advice/Recognized Authority**. Are you top of your field and can you prove it?
7. **Customization/Most Options**. How many options can you choose for your product?
8. **Speed**. How fast can you get your product to your clients?
9. **New and Unique**. Is your product unique or different or new?
10. **Strongest Guarantee**. What guarantee do you have that your competition will weep about?

(Jay, 2011, pp. 37-41)

Take some time out to brainstorm your USP and come up with a few to try out.

5. Media

This can be a very tricky area but is essential if you are to propel your business into the limelight it so deserves.

Whether its local national or international media, there are a few things that you need to bear in mind.

The media channels are desperate for good quality content with presentable, articulate people. You do not have to be a natural-born presenter but you do need to have good content, a message and be able to communicate effectively.

How do you get yourself in front of the media?

There are many different ways.

1. **Build a contacts list**. Create a list of media contacts, but be sure to update this regularly as they do change frequently.

2. **Build relationships**. If your local newspaper has a business or property correspondent, make sure you know who they are, introduce yourself and capture their direct contact details. Be that friendly local expert who can give them an opinion on stories that they may be struggling with.

3. **Know your deadlines**. Every media organisation works to deadlines and you need to know what they are. For example, your local radio station will have a morning and afternoon news show. Contact their newsdesks to ask for

their deadlines and aim to get your press release to the media 24 hours before you want it to be broadcast/ printed. You can embargo it to make sure they don't broadcast/print it before you want them to.

4. **Keep it short and simple**. Journalists work in a time-sensitive pressured environment. Make your press releases and your phone conversations with them precise, clear and easy to understand.

5. **Get attention**. Stories need to be eye-catching to both journalists and readers. Yours should be fresh and relevant and include at least one of these: a human interest angle, controversy, local personalities, a local angle, an unexpected event or pictures.

6. **Who is your audience**? Ask yourself what you really want the coverage to achieve. Do you want more clients? Names on a list or petition? Consumer action? You should aim to show how your issue affects the quality of people's lives where you live and offer positive solutions. Your business will then become a respected voice for change within your community.

7. **Sending your press release**. Construct a concise and attention grabbing press release and email it to your contacts. Copy it into the body of

an email and don't include logos or attachments as these are likely to bounce back.

8. **Follow it up!** Your press release has gone to all your contacts. Now you need to call them and ask if there's anything else they need to know. Newsrooms can be chaotic places and your email may not have been read. Be prepared to pitch your story over the phone and highlight the whens, where's, whys and whos.

9. **Prepare for an interview.** Identify your three most important messages, and practice these out loud in advance. Try to relax and remember your audience will not be specialists. They don't want to hear complex arguments but do want to know what's important about the issue and how it might affect them. Avoid jargon and think about how you can frame your message within issues that people are worried about. Plan in advance for any questions you're likely to be asked and don't be afraid to ask the journalist what the format of the interview will be in advance. Many interviews are pre-recorded and it is quite normal to ask for the recording to be stopped and ask for the question to be posed again if you make a mistake or are stuck. Most importantly be polite, be precise, be honest, be helpful and show your passion rather than expertise.

10. **Perseverance pays**. Don't be put off if your story doesn't get media coverage. You can always ask your local media contacts why they didn't cover it and use this advice to help construct future press releases. It could be something as simple as your story missing their deadline. Keep trying – local media relies on local stories and getting information from local organisations and groups. There are so many news channels out there that are desperate for content – makes yours the one they want!

8. Database segmentation

Many people have a set of clients or clients and do not understand why if they send out a mailing or promotion that it does not work as well as they'd expect it too.

Often it's because they are not segmenting their list.

A client can be valued at many different levels.

You can value a client on:

- The spend per product
- The spend per night
- The spend per month/year
- The lifetime spend

However by valuing a client just on spend, you do not take into account the time you need to invest into each client.

So you may wish to then look at segmenting clients by time invested or spent with them.

This may then bring out a different set of client segments for you to consider.

You may then have a matrix similar to this one:

Client Type	Spend	Time
Standard or Worst Client	Low	High
Silver Client but Time Required is Low	Low	Low
Gold Client but Requires Time	High	High
Premium or Best Client	High	Low

9. Vision statement

We discussed this at some length back in Chapter 4, 6 and 18.

Make sure you have a vision statement and share it with your staff, your peers, your mentor and your partners. Get their buy-in and then go do it!

Stage #4 of the 5 Stage Blueprint

Construct

STAGE #4 CONSTRUCT

Day 25: Systems

#4 – The Power of Construct

One of the tragic differences between a company that succeeds and is still around in ten or twenty years from now is in the quality and robustness of the construction of their systems.

This could be anything from a system for how we answer the phone, to how we make a sale, to how we input data onto a system through to how we deliver a product to our client.

Most people give little thought to these systems when they set up a business which is why they then get into the zone of "overwhelm" rather than being in the flow of creating and driving their business forward to meet the needs of their clients and suppliers.

Often this is because many entrepreneurs come from the employee or self-employee mindset of having to do everything themselves and not being able to trust anybody else to do the work for them. This generally leads to a control-freak type mentality without which the business cannot move forward and will stagnate as employees get frustrated with not being able to get on with their jobs nor being given responsibilities which can they can grow into overtime.

This is why when my 100K Club mentees come together, we go through a Systems-Down process to get them to think about how, when, where and what should we be doing at all times to deliver on our client promises.

And this is where we enter into the "construct" phase of our business in order to ensure that we build a business that can deliver added value whether you are there or not.

Let's share some examples.

An investor is looking for joint venture partners and sourcers to help her accelerate his portfolio. She attends four network meetings per month and on average collects around 10 cards per meeting. Currently she follows up with 3 out of 10 of these contacts through personal phone calls and emails.

A sourcer gets 20 property deals per month through contacts, leaflets and networking which he sends onto his database of 1,000 investors. He typically sells around 2 deals per month.

A landlord has 10 multi-let properties which due to lack of investment has around 8 vacancies per month. He succeeds in filling 4 out of 8 vacancies within 3 weeks and the other 4 take around 6 weeks meaning he always has vacancies.

And the list can continue.

The reason why the people in the above examples are not at the income levels they wish to be is due to their lack of systems and processes in place to automate many of their day-to-day activities.

Here are a few very simple examples of how they could turn around their fortunes within the next 30 days through using some easily-implemented process flows.

The investor could increase his contact rates by putting in place some processes.

Firstly capture three key pieces of data per new contact she meets on the back of the business card; speciality (ie sourcer, finance provider), what they are looking for and what the investor could help them with. She could then input these into either a spreadsheet or a simple system and then put a process in place to follow up with all of her new contacts the following day via email. Then follow up with these contacts 3 days later via phone.

Her contact rate would rise to 10/10 for email and approximately 6/10 for phone thus increasing her likelihood of meeting her portfolio targets.

The sourcer could rapidly improve his conversion rates through optimising his systems for contacting his clients.

Firstly he could identify his top 10% of clients and invite them to join his "VIP Club" ensuring that they get all deals 24 hours before anybody

else. Then he could use an email marketing programme to track who opens his emails and when and follow up with those who do with additional sales emails. He could also survey his clients to find out how they prefer him to contact them.

His deal conversion should go up to 4-6 per month just through implementing these simple changes.

The landlord could improve his profits and occupancy rates through better use of both maintenance and marketing systems.

Firstly he could identify a programme of maintenance works over the next 3 months which would give him quick wins (i.e. touch up a room, hide old sofa's with throws). Secondly he could then implement a tenant marketing and relationship system to identify twice the number of normal leads he gets (as this is a numbers game) and then enter these leads into a database so that he could keep in contact with them whether they take a room with him or not this time around. At the same time, he can send a simple newsletter out to his existing tenants informing them of the maintenance plan.

His room take-up should go to 6/7 out of 8 within 2 weeks and reduce the number of vacancies to 4 per month as the tenants should stay longer once they can see that work is being done

None of these processes and systems is rocket science but often the most capable people will become swamped in trying to do tasks that they are ill-suited to carry out or they will continue plodding along hoping to get themselves out of the mire that they have found themselves in.

Quick Win

STOP! STEP BACK! EVALUATE WHY ARE YOU DOING A TASK?

And ask yourself this question.

IS THERE A BETTER WAY? CAN I BUILD A PROCESS OR SYSTEM AROUND IT?

Systems are like the cogs in a car engine.

When you get in your car and you start driving, you generally have a destination (focus) in mind. You are the catalyst in getting there (people), and you may use maps or signs to help (marketing).

You'll certainly need money to put petrol in the engine (finance) but you are reliant upon the car's internal workings to get you there without breaking down (the system).

A business is similar to this. You can have the greatest vision, the greatest people, the greatest sales and marketing on earth but unless you have any form of robust systems you may find yourself failing because you do not have the consistency of systems in place to carry you through the times when the rest of the organisation fails - and systems is all you have to fall back on.

Your systems are a set of things, actions, ideas and information that interact with each other and in doing so, affect and alter other systems.

Gerber talks extensively about how systems will improve your organisation in his book The E-Myth Revisited, which I encourage you to read.

There are three types of system:

1) **Environmental**. These systems are put in place to manage your environment. They could dictate things such as the colour pattern in your office, your cleaning standards, the type of computers you use and the stationery products you favour. They are systems that allow you to focus upon the more important but fluid systems for daily human interaction.

2) **People**. These systems move you from A to B in a predefined route. They allow you to put systems in place to be completely focused upon delivery of your product or service through a predefined pattern which has been proven to be the optimum route. People systems could be used in sales, marketing, operations and finance - or anywhere needing a robust platform to operate.

3) **Information**. This brings all systems together to help us monitor and review them. It's similar to KPIs but from the perspective of each system that we put in place.

So we may monitor

Information	Benchmark
How many calls were made	1
How many prospects were reached	2
How many appointments /viewings were scheduled	3
How many appointments / viewings were confirmed	4
How many appointments / viewings were held	5
How many presentations were scheduled	6
And you would have the same for confirmed and held for each appointment or viewing	
How many products or services were sold	7
What was the average pound value	8

These should be collated digitally in a database to identify what is working and what needs attention.

This information will tell you the conversion rate between each benchmark in your system.

It will tell you where your people need help.

If you understand and know the cost of each benchmark, then it will indicate the true cost of making a sale.

Without this information you run the risk of running your business without understand how it works or how to improve it!

Sales Systems

A sales system is used in any format to generate more sales.

To identify the ideal sales system we need to focus upon:

a) Identifying specific decision points or benchmarks within the sales process
b) Scripting of the words that take you from each 'yes' point in the process
c) Creating the various materials to be used in the script (slides, hand-outs and visuals)
d) Memorising each decision point script
e) Delivering the script by salespeople in the exact fashion
f) Leaving the sales team to communicate more effectively by engaging with their prospect

The key with any sales system is:

1) Creating the appointment
2) Doing a needs analysis on the business or person we are selling to
3) Presenting a solution to the issues identified in the needs analysis

If we follow these steps there is no need to sell or to close but rather to walk the prospective client through the steps involved in order to offer them a solution to choose from in order to then move forward.

You can use this on any type of process which is designed to bring in more revenue. So whether this be sourcing, making appointments for viewings, finding new clients, use a sales system to improve your processes.

Below is an example of a system used to generate appointments for tenant viewings. Note that the first two points are a marketing process which we'll cover in the next section.

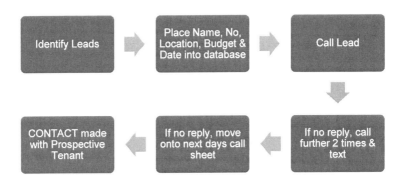

Marketing Systems

A marketing system is used in any format to generate more leads for the sales team to convert into sales.

To identify the optimum marketing system, we need to focus upon:

g) Identifying specific decision points or benchmarks within the marketing process
h) Scripting of the words or materials that take you from each 'yes' point in the process
i) Creating the various materials to be used in the script (i.e. slides, hand-outs and visuals)
j) Delivering the agreed process by marketing people in the same fashion
k) Leaving the marketing team to communicate more effectively by engaging with their prospect

Sometimes people drop the scripting part from the marketing process because more often than not they are dealing with less interaction.

For instance here is an example of a small process to generate tenant leads.

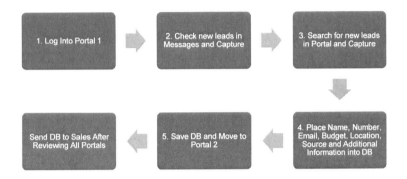

The key with any marketing system is

1) identifying where the leads come from
2) setting up appropriate lead generation systems to generate leads from these areas
3) having step-by-step processes in place so that anybody can generate the leads through following the system

If we follow these steps, then there is no need to have all of these processes handled by ourselves. We could outsource or delegate to somebody else. The aim is to capture as many prospective leads as possible in order to send to sales for qualification.

You can use this on any type of process which is designed to bring in more revenue.

Day 26: Finance

Imperative in any organisation is your finance function.

Without having dedicated personnel focusing upon receiving and paying funds as well as monitoring your run rates on cashflow, cash at bank and forecasting future performance is the difference between an also-ran and a future proof business.

The finance function doesn't need to be a full time person to begin with but having somebody on a part-time basis to allow you to focus on revenue generating activities is helpful as otherwise you will become bogged down in the minutiae of running your company rather than working on your company.

Main Finance Functions

So where do we begin with the main functions required to make finance work?

1) Accounts payable.

This is where our attention is upon what we have to pay out.

This could include contractors, insurance, legal fees, business purchases and so on.

2) Accounts receivable.

This is where our focus is upon what is going to be coming into the business.

This could include rents, finder's fees, letting fees, refinancing and property sales.

Key Performance Indicators (KPIs)

The key distinction in bringing the two of these together is having a financial forecast with Key Performance Indicators and reviewing progress on a regular basis.

Without this you are just counting numbers. And numbers generally don't excite people unless they are Sheldon Cooper (the madcap scientist in Big Bang Theory).

To begin with, here are some critical items that you need to be monitoring on a regular basis if you are in the business of renting properties:

1) Average rent (number of rents divided by properties, or total rent of house divided by rooms)

2) Lifetime rent (this may need to be estimated to begin with, so use 12 months for a single let and eight months for a multi-let)

3) Occupancy rate (number of properties or rooms available divided by properties or rooms currently rented)

4) Average rental arrears (average number of arrears experienced over the last three months)

5) Rental collection rate (rent collected versus the actual rent due over the last three months)

Depending on your business model, your KPIs could be very different.

The challenge here is to create 4-6 KPIs then keep monitoring them.

Client account

A client account is necessary in order to protect client monies from your main operating account.

Every business should really have this as at some point you will probably be dealing with client monies.

A client account allows you to protect monies which are not yours but which you are holding on behalf of your client in a separate deposit account which although linked to your current account is not counted under the same terms as your current account.

It is not possible to set up standing orders or direct debits on a client account as these funds are seen as protected funds. Neither will you be able to have any facilities on this account as in the bank's eyes, it's seen as a deposit account.

Speak to your bank to get one set up.

Regular Bank Reconciliation

Managing your money is a priority and you need to do this on a weekly basis.

Reconciliation is about what goes out versus what comes in, matching payments coming in with what is expected.

If we have a pipeline of rents to come in, then the reconciliation process is a case of ticking these off one-by-one and contacting tenant who have not paid.

You'll also have some unresolved reconciliations that need further work. These could include cash payments or amounts that do not seem to tally with the payments expected.

Putting in place a process to do this at least weekly will save you a lot of time and heartache in the future.

Bookkeeper

You have two choices when it comes to balancing your books. You can do it yourself, or hire a bookkeeper.

Keeping your books is essential in any business and is in most cases required by law. This involves the recording of financial transactions either manually into ledgers or on a computer.

To be good at keeping books, you'll need to be methodical, well organised, enjoy working through documents and seeing a set of figures add up.

The time required to be spent on your books will be dictated by the size of your business. At a minimum you'll need to record your income and expenditure every week, tallying receipts and recording your business mileage.

On top of this you may have VAT, PAYE, Corporation Tax and other items to record and pay.

I'd always recommend hiring a bookkeeper unless you find that this is your skillset. In that case you need to have people in your team who are focused on sales, marketing and operations.

You can find a qualified bookkeeper through referral or via an organisation such as bookkeepers.org.uk.

If you are going to do it yourself, make sure you fit this into your weekly plan - and do it consistently.

Accountant

An accountant is not necessary if you are a sole trader, or to some extent a limited liability partnership, but it is essential if you run a limited company.

An accountant is generally part of a firm of accountants whose role is varied but includes submitting your company return, dealing with issues such as tax, VAT and PAYE, and advising you on financial matters relating to your company.

To find a good accountant; get referrals. Here are some things to look out for based on my experience of working with accountants over the past 10 years:

- Make sure you are clear about what you are trying to achieve so you don't waste your time and money. What may be relevant for a company with 10 staff may not be relevant for your start-up. Ask what support they have in place for when you expand.

- Before you make any appointments, talk to three or four different accountancy firms. You'll want to get information about their charges including the initial consultation fee (if there is one), how they handle the longer term client relationship, and anything else important to you such as whether they are willing to come and see you in your own home or workplace.

- Ask about their qualifications. What they are, what they mean; ask how long the firm has been in business, and what your adviser specialises in.

- Ask about ways to pay charges and fees that might make it easier for you. I'm sure I don't need to tell you to negotiate a better deal or payment options that suit you better. You can pay monthly, quarterly or annually depending on the deal you strike. You might even get returns thrown in for free if you take up their PAYE service.

- As it's perfectly legal in the UK for anyone to set themselves up as an accountant, you should check that they have qualifications issued by one of the recognised bodies in the UK. The recognised bodes are varied but prominent ones include ICAEW, ICAS, CIMA or ACCA. You should be able to see certificates displayed in their offices.

Find out more

http://www.accaglobal.co.uk
http://www.icaew.com
http://icas.org.uk
http://www.ifa.org.uk
http://www.cimaglobal.com

As far as costs are concerned - how long is a piece of string? Based on experience I'd expect to pay anything from £750 to £1,250 per year for a firm of accountants to prepare the annual accounts and return them to Companies House.

Additional services such as VAT, PAYE, bookkeeping and tax advice will cost extra. Shop around and see what deal you can come to.

It's important you can work with your accountant, to know they will act in your best interests and are genuinely interested in working with you.

Contractors

It's important to keep on top of contractor payments both from a cashflow perspective and also to ensure that they are paid on time.

We therefore need a system to process their invoices.

At the very minimum you need a system which:

- Receives an invoice from a contractor
- Approves the payment
- Makes a payment to the contractor
- Checks to make sure these things have happened.

Contractors who are paid on time or before they expect will become loyal and trusted contractors.

We pay all contractors every Friday without fail provided that they submit an invoice by Wednesday afternoon.

Employees

From a Finance perspective, the main focus here will be upon the monthly payment of salary and expenses.

Depending on your company setup and how you pay employees will dictate the process you put in place for this but think about doing this on a set date in time every month.

We use the last Friday of the month to make payments out to employees.

We use this to process salary and expenses.

You can decide which expenses you'd like to pay but typically this will include items that employees have had to purchase in the line of their work such as stamps, parking and items for the business.

You'll also at this stage want to pay any mileage that you may be paying to mobile staff who because of their jobs have to travel. The prescribed amount you can pay up to for mileage is up to 45 pence for the first 10,000 miles and 25 pence per mile after this as of April 2013.

Cashflow

The final piece in the jigsaw for the Finance function is managing cashflow.

This is often done through Management Reporting on monies coming in, monies going out, and stock levels held (and value) together with a forecast for future sales.

Liabilities would also be held here in terms of bad debtors and depreciating stock (such as computers and perishable goods if any).

The Finance function will also want to manage the facilities of the company in terms of credit cards and overdrafts in order to ensure that it is not over exposed in borrowings or debts.

A Weekly Report should be shared with Senior Management so everyone is aware of where the business currently stands, what the challenges are and how the pipeline forecast directly impacts upon revenue growth and stability for the company.

Things To Consider

What are your KPI's? Write them down.

1	2
3	4

Have you set up a client account?	Yes	No
Are you doing the books or outsourcing?		
Do you have four accountants to speak to?		
Do you have a weekly bank reconciliation process?		
Do you have a contractor payment process?		
Do you have an employee payment process?		

What management reports will you put in place to manage cashflow?

Finance Systems

We've discussed most of the systems you will need for Finance in the chapter of that name, but don't forget to actually take some time to think about these systems.

Finance is an easy one to forget about but this is where all of the monies are counted and allows you to see how profitable or unprofitable your activities are. Make sure you therefore look at this area in the same detail as Sales and Marketing systems.

What environment systems do you believe that you will need to have?

What people systems do you believe that you will need to have?

What information systems do you believe you will need to have?

What sales systems need work?

What marketing systems need work?

What finance systems should you put in place?

Stage #5 of the 5 Stage Blueprint

Conquer

STAGE #5: CONQUER

Day 27 – The Power of Conquer

When all is said and done, there's a big difference between a company that's struggling and one that's on top of its game.

I really want you to be one of those companies that's ahead of the curve and on top of the game of business.

You see for me, there's no better feeling than knowing that everything you've been working towards will culminate in you being positioned as one of the top five companies in your area for the industry you're focused on – maybe even one of the top five companies in your country. In fact, lets not stop there – why not focus on being the number one company wherever you are?

Getting to expert position within your chosen strategy, field or industry takes time but you can do it quickly by shortcutting what most people do and focus on the end result.

How do you do this?

Let me illustrate this with a story.

Back in 2010, I had just started Millennia Property with two other directors.

We had already opened two offices and then we started getting approached by other investors wanting to get into what we were doing and replicate our success.

We had people wanting to pay us £3,000, £7,000, £10,000 and even £30,000 to learn what we had done and how they could do it themselves. Then we started getting joint venture introductions for investors who wanted to replicate our business model and run their own "franchise-type" business with sums of anything from £35,000 to £80,000 being discussed.

One of the chief reasons we had so many people contact us is that we had used expert positioning within the market place to rapidly launch each of our business units and start to dominate the local market place. This was primarily done through a bespoke launch plan coupled on with a phenomenal marketing, sales and finance machine.

The results were incredible with one business unit going from 34 units to 180 units within 12 months of the business starting. Now not every business was this successful but this was partly because they didn't follow the launch plan and systems to the letter.

The importance of this lesson is – don't deviate from the plan and think you know better; just embrace the plan and go with it and the money will arrive.

Most businesses never make it past stage #1 of the blueprint; they don't truly understand where they are going and what they are focused on.

If you're one of the exclusive 2% of business owners who do truly get this, then there is hope for you. And it's by following a proven model where your business truly begins to accelerate and grow to six figures.

As human beings, we are naturally competitive creatures stemming from our old pack days of being in a tribe and a village and wanting to conquer other villages, lands and countries!

It strikes me as crazy that when somebody starts up in business, they

- Expect people just to turn up
- Expect people just to buy without really knowing what they are buying
- Expect people to start raving about them
- Expect to have press and media attention on them
- Expect that their product or service is the best
- Expect to start making profits from day one

This kind of thinking is dangerous and whilst I'm a fan of the "ready, fire, aim" method of launching products, services and businesses – to a degree we need to acknowledge that in today's media-saturated world of 24 hour broadcasting, social media, advertising and intrusion into our life that to stand out and make a difference is more difficult than it was even 10 years ago.

Now is the time of standing apart.

- People turn up because they've heard about us through multiple methods of advertising

- People buy because our products or services are precise, targeted and aimed at solving their problems
- People rave about us because we deliver impeccable service and extraordinary client attention
- People get to know us through the media because we've followed a strategic launch plan that works
- People will kick and scream and be vocal about getting hold of our product first because they know how good it is and what their life will be like if they don't have it
- We start to make profits within 1-7 days of launching our product, 7-21 days of launching our service and 90 days of launching our business.

Don't settle for second best; aim to be the best of the best.

Quick Win.

Think of three businesses that you admire that are in your sector. What do they do? How are they known? What do they advertise? How can you replicate their success?

Can you "plan" your success?

Launch plan

Pulling all of this together requires a launch plan.

Whenever I launch a new business – I use my 90 Day Blast Off Plan to launch the business.

Doing all of this can be quite traumatic if you've not done it before and there is a tendency to miss things and overdo some elements because you prefer them or they fit with you more so than other elements of the overall business.

Things to consider on any launch plan are the following:

When are you going to officially launch?
What collateral do you need in place to launch?
What's your story? What's your message? What's different?
What training needs to take place before launch?
What research do you need to do?
Who do you need to meet to get buzz created about the launch?
What social media channels should you use?
Which government organisations can you contact?
What advertising can be done locally?
What sales targets are in place?
What systems are already in place?
What's your budget for the launch?
What insurance, equipment, stationery, office, telephones are in place?
What affiliates do you have in place?
Where's the launch party going to be?

Have you told the press?

Typically these activities will be concentrated within the first four weeks but there is follow on activities over a three-month period to ensure that you are firmly ensconced in the local market and becoming a major player.

Create a plan and then launch your business!

FINAL REMARKS

Day 28: Review and Preparation

So we are nearly at the end of our time together in these first 30 days. **Congratulations.**

You are among the 1% who know 80% more than most property investors out there about how to build a property business.

Now there are some items we need to review.

This is what I like to call your **outcome hit list**. I know you've been busy over these last 28 days working through the book but we are nearly there and I need your full attention and dedication to finish what we've started together.

The outcome hit list is a one-page summary of tasks to get you thinking about the things you need to have in place to ensure you've done everything and that you are ready to get cracking right away.

This isn't going to take you more than about 5 minutes to do. You may need to refer back to earlier chapters in order to ensure that you have completed some of these tasks.

Once you've completed the outcome hit list exercise, you're done for the day. Tomorrow I'll be sharing the next steps with you.

THE OUTCOME HIT LIST

☐ Do you have a reason why you are in property?

☐ Do you have a map to get from A to Z?

☐ Do you have a vision that excites you?

☐ Have you chosen two strategies?

☐ Do you have a 12x4 Plan?

☐ Have you put in place a weekly planning session?

☐ Are you following the daily Outcome Planner?

☐ Have you set up your business?

☐ Have you got a business name?

☐ Have you got a bank account?

☐ Have you got a work space?

☐ Have you got a USP?

☐ Have you got a business plan?

☐ Have you identified two networking sessions to attend?

☐ Have you got an organisation chart?

☐ Have you put in place basic Operational flow charts?

☐ Do you have two sales strategies that you are following?

☐ Do you have two marketing strategies that you are following?

☐ Have you got a launch plan?

☐ Do you have at least three KPIs?

☐ Have you created at least one system?

☐ Have you hired or advertised for a person to help you?

If you've completed these, give yourself a big pat on the back.

You rock!

Otherwise, go back and do them now!

Day 29: The Next Steps

We are now nearly at the end of our journey together - at least for now.

It's a great time to reflect on what you've learned, and what you are going to do to take your business forward.

Do you clearly understand your life plan now? This is really the foundation for getting going.

Have you got a plan that excites you and gets you going?

Have you chosen two strategies that are going to make your business a huge success?

Now is the time to take action and on this final day reflect on what you've learnt.

Here's some questions to ponder:

What is your most important takeaway from this book?

What is the most challenging issue I have to overcome in order to achieve my life plan?

How am I going to change my life in order that I can achieve my dreams?

What will I miss if I don't take action?

Day 30: The End Game

Focus

Often people get started in the property game with a lot of passion, a lot of enthusiasm and a desire to succeed.

Property, like business and life in general, is not an easy game.

It's a game that needs to be played to win.

That's the difference between somebody who just cruises through the steps illustrated in the book versus someone who actively engages and works with each exercise to define their plan, their goals, their outcome and their life plan in conjunction with their desire to crack the property code.

There are many facets to the property game and at first it can be bewildering, but it is has been my intent and focus throughout this book to illustrate how you can set up a property business of your own that will allow you to succeed and achieve your ideal outcomes.

The code is not something that can be picked up overnight.

It's something that with careful preparation, education and support can be cracked within 12 months and allows you to set yourself up with a fun, profitable and sustainable business.

If you've not done the exercises, I'd highly recommend that you go back and do them. I designed my book in a way that you will get the most out by taking some time out each day to focus on an aspect of the property business that you absolutely need to know, and to work within this framework to develop your own business plan, outcome and strategies.

By now, you should have a firm understanding of:

- How to set up a business (whether property or outside the sector)
- How to market for new clients
- How to set up your organisation to deliver cost-effective service
- How to generate new sales every month
- How to manage your profit and loss account
- How to create systems that work for you
- How to create an operational framework attracting the right people
- The 45 different strategies you could pursue in the property arena
- How to actively implement these strategies into your business

I hope that the case studies inspired you to take action.

I hope that you have chosen at least TWO strategies to focus on and that you will go onto develop and focus upon these strategies further.

I hope that you've identified further learning and support strategies that resonate with you and that you feel that will benefit you and add to your knowledge and grasp of the strategies.

I hope that you've reached the end of the book and feel that you've learn something new, relearned something old, but most of all you're excited about how no matter how young or old you are, you can achieve your desired outcome by taking action today.

You are the only person stopping yourself from achieving your dreams so I urge you to follow them today, not tomorrow and start taking massive action.

Have a dream that is backed by a daily ritual of achieving results that have a purpose and that you have taken action on.

Now is the time to step up and be counted; to create a business that you can truly be proud of and that leaves a legacy to our future.

Think of this as a stepping stone to the future. We don't know what's going to happen but you can be certain that the world in 20 years will be different to the world today and it's those that have a vision, a plan and a purpose that will be light years ahead of the flock.

I've been in business for nearly 20 years now and in my lifetime I've seen the rise of computers, mobile phones, satellite navigation, tablets, internet, microwaves, wi-fi, apps, email, spam, low-cost airlines and so much more.

What's going to happen in the next 20 years – mobile marketing, products-on-demand, 3D printing, human augmentation of technology, the rise of the aware machine, a colony on Mars – who knows?

My wish for you is that you got a huge benefit from reading this report and that you will act upon it quickly.

If you do nothing else, do these five things

1. Get really really CLEAR on your vision for your life and how property can help you with this

2. Create a business with one firm strategy in mind

3. Create a client-centric model where clients come first and profits come second

4. Construct world-class systems that allow you to compete with the best companies on earth

5. Dominate your market, dominate your industry; conquer all who come before you.

Good luck. And may your vision become reality, your dreams become real and your businesses be super-successful so you can start to move to the next stage of the blueprint (The 4.5 Advanced Stage Blueprint to Mastering Your 7 Figure Business).

I would love to hear of your success stories and your comments on my book.

If you can spare the time to send me a few lines telling me what you thought of the book, sharing a particular success story or a testimonial, please drop me a line at itookaction@crackingthepropertycode.com .

To your continued success

Results + Purpose + Action = Your Dreams Becoming Your Life

Matthew Moody
Northamptonshire
March 2017

P.S. To get a free download of my 100K Club webinar where I share the reasons why you need to be thinking about building a 6 Figure business and how you can do it quite quickly this year; just go to this private download link

www.crackingthepropertycode.com/bookbonuses101

Bibliography

Brinkley, M. (1999). *The House Builders Bible: Millennium Edition.* Cambridge: Rodelia.

Davidson, H. (1997). *Even More Offensive Marketing.* London: Penguin.

Denny, R. (1997). *Selling To Win.* London: Kogan Page.

Dunn, J. (2013, April 05). *36 Social Rules For Social Media.* Retrieved May 08, 2013, from Edudemic: http://edudemic.com/2013/04/the-36-rules-of-social-media/

Gerber, M. E. (1995). *The Emyth Revised:Why Most Small Business Don't Work and What to do About It.* New York: Harper Business.

Harrison, F. (2005). *Boom Bust, House Prices, Banking and The Depression of 2010 - Is Your Hmoe At Risk?* London: Shepheard-Walwyn.

Hatch, J. (2012). Kickstart Your Social Media Marketing. *Small Business Success Tour 2012* (p. 32). London: Infusionsoft.

Humphreys, J. (2011). *Authority Black Book.* Retrieved from Authority Black Book: http://www.authorityblackbook.com/

Jay, J. (2011). *Overnight Success: 21 Sales and Marketing Secrets.* Chatham: CPI Mackays.

Lacoma, T. (2012, November 9). *How Many New Businesses Fail in the First Year.* Retrieved May 21, 2013, from eHow: http://www.ehow.co.uk/how-does_5212542_many-businesses-fail-first-year_.html

Pew Research Center. (Feb 2005, Aug 2006, May 2008, April 2009, May 2010, May 2011). *Internet & American Life Project surveys.*

Robbins, A. (n.d.). The Time Of Your Life.

Simister, P. (2009, 03 22). *Dominos Pizza USP: Model It To Develop Your Own.* Retrieved May 21, 2013, from Small Business Marketing: http://businesscoaching.typepad.com/small_business_marketing/2009/03/dominos-pizza-usp-model-it-to-develop-your-own.html

Recommended Further Reading

Avins,P. (2009). *Business SOS: Proven, Fast-Acting Strategies to Take Your Business From Surviving to Thriving.* Marsh Gibbon: Paul Avins Enterprises

Carter, D. (2008). *SPLAM! Successful Property Letting and Management.* Dorset: Tracker Dog Media

Conran Levinson, J. (2003).*Guerilla Marketing for Free.* New York: Houghton Mifflin Company

De Roos, D (2001). *Real Estate Riches: How to Become Rich Using Your Banker's Money.* New York: Warner Books

De Roos, D. (2002). *101 Ways to Massively Increase The Value of Your Real Estate Without Spending Much Money.* New York: Time Warner Inc.

De Roos, D. (2004). *Making Money in Real Estate: Smart Steps to Building Your Wealth Through Property.* New Jersey: John Wiley & Sons

Hamilton, R.(2006). *Your Life Your Legacy: An Entreprenuers Guide to Finding Your Flow.* Surrey: Achievers International.

Lawrenson,D. (2009). *Successful Property Letting:How to Make Money in Buy-to-Let.* London: Constable and Robinson

McElroy,K. (2008). *The Advanced Guide to Real Estate Investing: How to Identify The Hottest Markets And Secure The Best Deals.* New York: Grand Central Publishing

Shaw, A. (2006). *Money For Nothing And Your Property For Free: The Psychology of Property Investing And How to Apply it The Easy Way or The Really Easy Way!* Brighton: Andy Shaw

Torrisi, P. (2008). *The Apprentice Property Master.* Oxford: Spring Hill

Wagner,D. (2012). *The Expert Success Formula.*

Walton, C. (2011). *Peak Performance in 60 Seconds: The 4 Essentials to Maximise Your Energy, Resilience and Performance.* London: Awaken Books.

About Wealth Success Alliance

Wealth Success Alliance is the exclusive club for property investors who want to build a six figure business. We play to win, we play to give back and we play so we can leave a legacy.

Founded by Matthew Moody in 2012, our mission is to:

- Build a million homes through global joint ventures
- Educate, train and mentor 1,000 business owners and property investors to become millionaires
- Create a change in the law and regulations to foster a more fluid approach to tenure, income and debt
- Create an educational institute that offers entrepreneurship, investment and business training
- Have a lot of fun through shared experiences, memorable events and lifelong friends in business.

Remember we only have one life so dream big and go take that next step.

Make More Money | Have More Fun | Give More Back

www.wealthsuccessalliance.co.uk

Further Products and Services

Over the years investing in property and building businesses has become second nature to me. The following shows products and services you may wish to consider if you are looking for a mentor, furniture, property management or a workshop.

Websites

www.yourhmoexpert.com is the leading authority site for HMOs UK loaded with strategies, audio and videos.

www.matthewmoody.co.uk is my speaker site and is where you can contact me to speak at your event.

www.hmofurniturepackages.com is where to go for quality furnishings for your property but at an affordable price.

www.stanfordknightsletting.com is for property management and investment in Northamptonshire.

Connect with me on Social Media

 YourHMOExpert

 matthewjmoody

 matthew-moody

About The Author

Matthew Moody has been investing in property since

2004 and been involved in the HMO market, educating, sourcing, management and coaching for 13 years.

From humble beginnings in Hull as the son of a policeman, he studied Theology at Oxford University, then went onto manage the European pricing and inventory functions for major corporations including Europcar and RCI. After being inspired in 2003 to take massive action, he now owns a cashflow-rich property portfolio of £3.5 million properties (the majority 6 bed+ HMOs) and was instrumental in his last business (Millennia Property) winning Letting Agent of the Year in 2010, managing over 600 units of property and taking control of over £16.5 million pounds worth of property through instalment contracts and long leases.

His mission is to make a difference in the property and business world and show people that you don't have to struggle; you need to take the right action step-by-step to truly live out your dreams.

Discover your outcome, prioritize your life and take massive action today!